MASTERY STUDY GUIDE

Macroeconomics:
Principles and Applications

Second Edition

Robert E. Hall
Department of Economics
Stanford University

Marc Lieberman
Department of Economics
New York University

Prepared by
Geoffrey A. Jehle
Department of Economics
Vassar College

SOUTH-WESTERN
THOMSON LEARNING

Australia · Canada · Mexico · Singapore · Spain · United Kingdom · United States

Mastery Study Guide for Macroeconomics: Principles and Applications, 2e, by Robert E. Hall and Marc Lieberman. Prepared by Geoffrey A. Jehle.

Vice President/Team Director: Jack W. Calhoun
Senior Developmental Editor: Dennis Hanseman
Senior Marketing Manager: Lisa L. Lysne
Production Manager: Sharon L. Smith
Manufacturing Coordinator: Charlene Taylor
Cover Design: Paul Neff Design
Printer: Globus Printing

Printed in the United States
1 2 3 4 5 6 04 03 02 01 00

For more information contact South-Western College Publishing, 5101 Madison Road, Cincinnati, Ohio, 45227, or find us on the Internet at http://www.swcollege.com

For permission to use material from this product, contact us by
• **telephone: 1-800-730-2214**
• **fax: 1-800-730-2215**
• **web: http://www.thomsonrights.com**

ISBN: 0-324-01960-2

PREFACE

There is a secret to learning economics. Those who discover the secret learn economics more quickly, understand it more deeply, and do better on exams than those who do not. The secret is this: Economics must be learned actively, not passively.

Passive learning relies on "taking things in." Merely listening to your professor, reading the book, flipping through your notes, and feeling like you "get it" because it all makes sense when someone else says it—these are the hallmarks of passive learning. While passive learning can work in some subjects, generations of students have discovered it does not work very well in economics.

Active learning, by contrast, works very well in economics. Active learning means periodically closing your book, closing your notes, and reproducing the material on your own. It means knowing how to *use* the vocabulary of economics—not just recognizing terms when you hear them. It means drawing graphs on your own, explaining what happens as we move along a curve, and what makes a curve shift—not just making sense of a graph when someone else draws it for you. It means solving problems from the ground up—not just following along as someone else solves them for you.

This Mastery Study Guide will help you to study economics actively. Other than this preface, you will find nothing here for you to just read, review, or "take in." As soon as you turn the page, you will be asked to *do* things—again and again and again.

Each chapter of this study guide corresponds to the same numbered chapter in Hall and Lieberman's *Macroeconomics: Principles and Applications, 2nd edition*. Every chapter includes the following sections:

- *Speaking Economics* asks you to fill in key vocabulary terms when you are given their definitions;

- *Chapter Highlights* asks you to identify missing parts of important conclusions from the text;

- *Important Concepts* asks you to provide lists and brief explanations about central ideas in the text;

- *Skills and Tools* gives you practice solving quantitative problems and using graphs—plotting them, interpreting them, and drawing conclusions from them;

- *Practice Tests* offer multiple choice and true/false questions to help you decide when you've mastered a chapter of the text, and when you need to go back and review.

In many ways, learning economics is like learning to play a musical instrument. At first your fingers are stiff and even the simplest movement seems labored and unfamiliar. But with active practice—and more active practice!—things soon become natural and easy, until you can scarcely believe you ever had trouble at all. I hope this Mastery Study Guide helps you make that transition, and helps you become a "natural" in economics.

TO THE INSTRUCTOR

Nothing is more frustrating than inconsistency between a textbook and its associated study guide. I know this firsthand. Over the years, I've suffered—as have my students—with study guides and texts that seem to come from different planets.

In writing this Mastery Study Guide, I've worked closely with the textbook's authors, Bob Hall and Marc Lieberman, to ensure complete consistency in approach, language, and content. Indeed, the authors themselves contributed many of the questions and problems in this guide. From the beginning our goal was to make the transition from text to study guide—and back again—as seamless as possible.

ACKNOWLEDGEMENTS

Bob Hall and Marc Lieberman have written a gem of a text, and it was a pleasure to prepare this Mastery Study Guide with them. Their devotion to their subject, and to their reader, is inspiring. Andrew Lemon, my assistant at Vassar College, worked above and beyond the call to meet our deadlines—checking, correcting, and suggesting problems, and always reminding us of the student's perspective.

Geoffrey A. Jehle
Poughkeepsie, New York

Contents

Answers to Questions

CHAPTER 1

WHAT IS ECONOMICS?

SPEAKING ECONOMICS

Fill in each blank with the appropriate word or phrase from the list provided in the word bank. (For a challenge, fill in as many blanks as you can *without* using the word bank.)

ECONOMICS 1. The study of choice under conditions of scarcity.

SCARCITY 2. A situation in which the amount of something available is insufficient to satisfy the desire for it.

Resources 3. The land, labor, and capital that are used to produce goods and services.

LABOR 4. The time human beings spend producing goods and services.

physical capital 5. Long-lasting tools used in producing goods and services.

Human capital 6. The skills and training of the labor force.

LAND 7. The physical space on which production occurs, and the natural resources that come with it.

microeconomics 8. The study of the behavior of individual households, firms, and governments, the choices they make, and their interaction in specific markets.

macroeconomics 9. The study of the economy as a whole.

positive econ. 10. The study of what *is*; of how the economy works.

normative econ. 11. The study of what *should be*, it is used to make value judgments, identify problems, and prescribe solutions.

model 12. An abstract representation of reality.

simplifying assump. 13. Any assumption that makes a model simpler without affecting any of its important conclusions.

critical assump. 14. Any assumption that affects the conclusions of a model in an important way.

1

Word Bank

capital   microeconomics
critical assumption   model
economics   normative economics
human capital   positive economics
labor   resources
land   scarcity
macroeconomics   simplifying assumption

CHAPTER HIGHLIGHTS

Fill in the blanks with the appropriate words or phrases. If you have difficulty, review the chapter and then try again.

1. Economics is the study of choice under conditions of ___scarcity___.

2. Society's problem is a scarcity of ___resources___.

3. Economists generally classify resources into three categories: ___LAND___, ___LABOR___, and ___CAPITAL___.

4. ___MICRO___ economics takes a close-up view of the economy, and is concerned with the behavior of *individual* actors on the economic scene.

5. ___MACRO___ economics deals with the overall economy, and focuses on variables like total output, total employment, and the general level of interest rates.

6. ___Positive___ economics deals with what *is*—with *how* the economy works.

7. ___Normative___ economics concerns itself with what *should be*. It is used to make judgments about the economy, identify problems, and prescribe solutions.

8. To understand the economy, economists make extensive use of *models*, which are ___abstract___ representations of reality.

9. A simplifying assumption is a way of making a model simpler, without changing any of its important ___conclusions___.

10. A ___critical___ assumption is an assumption that affects the conclusions of a model in important ways.

IMPORTANT CONCEPTS

Write a brief answer below each of the following items.

1. State whether each of the following questions is primarily microeconomic or macroeconomic, and whether it is primarily positive or normative. Don't worry about the answers to the questions—just classify them. (For example, the first question is a microeconomic, positive question.)

   a. If the price of compact discs rises, what will happen to the equilibrium price of cassette tapes?

   micro   *positive*

   b. If we raise the social security tax on wages and salaries, what will happen to total employment in the United States?

   macro   *positive*

   c. How much have pollution-control devices raised the price of automobiles?

   macro   *positive*

   d. Should the federal government use our tax dollars to support the arts?

   macro   *normative*

   e. What policies would help improve the average standard of living in less-developed countries?

   macro   *positive*

   f. Should less-developed countries like Ethiopia or Ghana use government funds to subsidize basic necessities like bread or milk?

   macro   *norm*

   g. Which is worse for society: a one percentage-point rise in the unemployment rate, or a one percentage-point rise in the inflation rate?

   macro   *norm*

2. Each of the following is an example of one of the three categories of resources. In the blanks, identify the categories.

   a. A surgeon's time in performing an operation   *LABOR*

   b. The surgeon's scalpel   *P CAPITAL*

   c. The surgeon's skills and training   *H CAPITAL*

   d. The iron ore used to make steel   *RESOURCES – LAND*

   e. The workers who make steel out of iron ore   *LABOR*

   f. The factory in which iron ore is made into steel   *CAPITAL*

   g. The services performed by a waiter at a restaurant   *LABOR*

   h. A restaurant's pots, pans and dishes   *CAPITAL*

Indicate whether the following statements are true or false, and then explain briefly.

3. "The more details we include in a model, the better the model will work."

    FALSE   model is supposed to simplify something

4. Economists make two types of assumptions in their economics models: positive assumptions and normative assumptions.

    F   simplifying, critical assumptions

SKILLS AND TOOLS

Note to the Student: Some of the basic principles of graphs and graphing are reviewed in the Appendix to Chapter 1 in your text. If it has been a while since you used graphs you might want to take a look at that section of the text before you do these exercises. Those already comfortable with graphs can proceed with the exercises.

For each of the following items, write the correct answer in the blank or circle the correct answer.

1. This table reports estimates of the United States' population (in millions) each year during the 1980s. The data are population in millions by year.

Year	US Population
1980	228
1981	230
1982	233
1983	235
1984	237
1985	239
1986	242
1987	244
1988	246
1989	248

US Population (millions)

   a. On the axes provided, carefully plot the data from the table.

   b. Looking at your graph in (1), which of the following best describes how population changed in the 1980s? _____
        i. Population generally decreased over the decade.
       ii. Population stayed roughly constant over the decade.
      iii. Population increased and decreased erratically over the decade.
      (iv.) Population increased at a roughly constant rate over the decade.

c. On your graph for (1) use a ruler and draw in a single straight line which seems to best fit the data you plotted.

d. Slope measures the rate of change in the y-axis variable for a one unit change in the x-axis variable. Bearing this in mind, what is the rate at which population changed over the decade of the 1980s? _20 mill/yr_

$$\frac{248-228}{10} = \frac{20}{1}$$

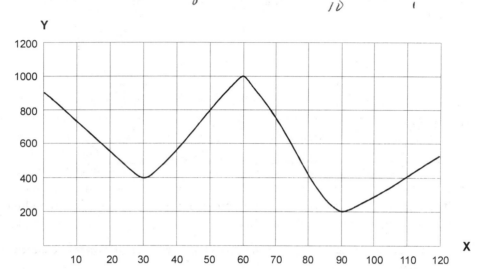

2. Study the graph in the preceding figure.

a. In the figure, Y increases when X increases from _____30_____ to _____60_____, and then again when X increases from _____90_____ to ____120____. In these two regions, the slope of the relationship between X and Y is (positive/negative/zero).

b. In the same figure, Y decreases when X increases from _____0_____ to _____30_____, and then again when X increases from ____60____ to _____90_____. In these two regions, the slope of the relationship between X and Y is (positive/negative/zero).

c. Y reaches its maximum value of ____1000____ when X has the value _____60_____. Y reaches its minimum value of ____200____ when X has the value ____90____.

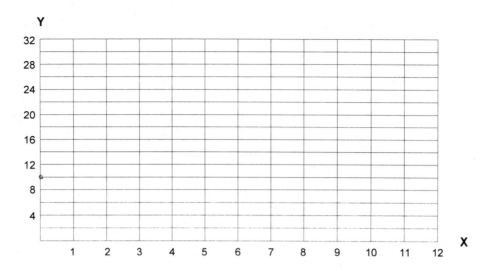

3. Graph each of the following equations on the grid provided. Then describe your graph by filling in the blanks.

a. Y = 2X + 10

This graph has a vertical intercept of _____ /0 _____ and a constant slope of _____ 2 _____ . As X increases, Y always (increases/decreases) at a (constant/changing) rate.

b. Y = 2X + 5

This graph has a vertical intercept of _____ 5 _____ and a constant slope of _____ 2 _____ . As X increases, Y always (increases/decreases) at a (constant/changing) rate.

c. Y = X + 10

This graph has a vertical intercept of _____ /0 _____ and a constant slope of _____ / _____ . As X increases, Y always (increases/decreases) at a (constant/changing) rate.

d. Y = 30 – 5X

This graph has a vertical intercept of _____ 30 _____ and a constant slope of _____ –5 _____ . As X increases, Y always (increases/decreases) at a (constant/changing) rate.

e. Y = 30 – 3X

This graph has a vertical intercept of _____ 30 _____ and a constant slope of _____ –3 _____ . As X increases, Y always (increases/decreases) at a (constant/changing) rate.

10-MINUTE PRACTICE TEST

Set a timer, giving yourself just ten minutes to answer all of the following questions. To see what you *really* know and remember, take the test at least a day *after* you've read the chapter in the text and completed the exercises in this study guide.

Multiple Choice: Circle the letter in front of the single best answer.

1. Economics can be defined as the study of
   a. business firms and how they can increase their profit.
   b. financial markets, like the stock market and the bond market.
   c. choice under conditions of scarcity.
   d. how households allocate their income to different uses.
   e. how businesses and government agencies allocate their revenue to different uses.

2. *Micro*economics studies the economic behavior of
   a. very small nations.
   b. very small people.
   c. individual businesses only.
   d. individual households only.
   e. individual decision-makers, including households and businesses.

3. Which of the following is a *resource,* from society's point of view?
   a. Meat
   b. Clothing
   c. The income tax
   d. An office building
   e. Electricity

4. Regardless of its truth or falsehood, the statement "A tax cut will cause faster growth in total output than an increase in government spending" is an example of
   a. positive microeconomics.
   b. positive macroeconomics.
   c. normative microeconomics.
   d. normative macroeconomics.
   e. none of the above.

5. Which of the following is the best example of a *model*?
   a. A dollar bill
   b. A coffee cup
   c. A drawing of a house
   d. A stop sign
   e. A laptop computer

6. The best way to study economics is
   a. *passively*, reading the book over and over again until you can follow the logical flow.
   b. *actively*, making sure you can reproduce the material on your own.
   c. with a phone in one hand and a remote control in the other.
   d. bent at the waist, making a 90-degree angle with your upper torso.
   e. with Country-and-Western music in the background.

True/False: For each of the following statements, circle T if the statement is true or F if the statement is false.

 T (F) 1. All assumptions in an economic model are *simplifying* assumptions.

T (F) 2. Economists classify resources into three categories: labor, physical capital and human capital.

T (F) 3. Normative economics deals with how the economy normally functions in ordinary times.

(T) F 4. In economics, we assume that individuals face scarcities of time and spending power.

(T) (F) 5. *Macro*economics studies the economies of large, industrialized nations, such as the United States or Japan.

CHAPTER 2

SCARCITY, CHOICE, AND ECONOMIC SYSTEMS

SPEAKING ECONOMICS

Fill in each blank with the appropriate word or phrase from the list provided in the word bank. (For a challenge, fill in as many blanks as you can *without* using the word bank.)

opp. cost   1. What we sacrifice when taking an action.

PPF   2. A curve showing all combinations of two goods that can be produced with the resources and technology currently available.

law of ↑ opp. cost   3. The more of something we produce, the more we must sacrifice to produce one more unit.

prod. ineff. *~~abs advantage~~*   4. A situation in which we could produce more of one good without sacrificing production of any other good.

specialized prod.   5. A method of production in which each person concentrates on a limited number of activities.

exchange   6. The act of trading with others to obtain what we desire.

abs advant   7. The ability to produce a good or service using *fewer resources* than other producers use.

comp. adv.   8. The ability to produce a good or service at a *lower opportunity cost* than other producers.

res. allocation   9. The determination of which goods and services are produced, how they are produced, and who gets them.

trad. econ.   10. An economy in which resources are allocated according to long-lived practices from the past.

command, centrally planned econ.   11. Two names for an economic system in which resources are allocated according to explicit instructions from a central authority.

market econ
~~_capitalism_~~ _____ 12. An economic system in which resources are allocated through individual decision making.

market _____ 13. A group of buyers and sellers with the potential to trade with one another.

price _____ 14. The amount of money that must be paid to a seller to obtain a good or service.

communism _____ 15. Communal ownership of most resources.

socalism _____ 16. State ownership of most resources.

capitalism _____ 17. Private ownership of most resources.

economic system 18. A system of resource allocation and resource ownership.

Word Bank

absolute advantage
capitalism
centrally planned economy
command economy
communism
comparative advantage
economic system
exchange
law of increasing opportunity cost
market

market economy
opportunity cost
price
production possibilities frontier (PPF)
resource allocation
socialism
specialization
productive inefficiency
traditional economy

CHAPTER HIGHLIGHTS

Fill in the blanks with the appropriate words or phrases. If you have difficulty, review the chapter and then try again.

1. The _opp. cost_ of any choice is all that we give up when we make that choice.

2. All production carries an _opp. cost_ : to produce more of one thing, society must shift _resources_ away from producing something else.

3. The law of _~~opp.~~ increasing_ opportunity cost tells us that the more of something we produce, the _greater_ is the opportunity cost of producing still more.

4. A firm, industry or an entire economy is productively _inefficient_ if it could produce more of some good without pulling resources from the production of any other good.

5. _Specialization_ and _Exchange_ enable us to enjoy greater production and higher living standards than would otherwise be possible. As a result, all economies exhibit high degrees of _Specialization_ and _Exchange_.

6. A person has a (an) _absolute advantage_ in producing some good if he or she can produce it using fewer resources than another person can.

7. A person has a (an) _comparative advantage_ in producing some good if he or she can produce it with a smaller opportunity cost than some other person can.

8. Total production of every good or service will be greatest when individuals specialize according to their _comp. advantage_

9. In a _central/command_ economy, resources are allocated by explicit instructions from some higher authority.

10. In a _~~capital~~ market_ economy, resources are allocated through individual decision making.

IMPORTANT CONCEPTS

Write a brief answer below each of the following questions.

1. Indicate whether the following statement is true or false, and then explain briefly: To determine the opportunity cost of a year of college, we would add the direct money cost and the income foregone. Thus, for someone who could have earned $30,000 as a full-time fisherman during the year, or $45,000 as a full-time truck driver that year, or $20,000 as a full-time tour guide that year, the opportunity cost would be the direct money cost plus a total income foregone of $30,000 + $45,000 + $20,000 = $95,000."

F

2. What economic law gives the production possibilities frontier its characteristic concave (upside-down bowl) shape?

    law of increasing opp. cost

3. Name two types of economic situations in which a "free lunch" for society might be possible.

   a. PROD. INEFF.

   b. RECESSION

4. List three separate reasons why specialization and exchange can lead to increased production.

   a.

   b.

   c.

5. College professors can usually locate books and articles in their college library faster than students. Yet most college professors hire students to find these materials. Is this consistent with the idea of comparative advantage? Briefly, why or why not?

6. List the three methods of resource allocation.

   a.

   b.

   c.

7. List the three methods of resource ownership.

   a.

   b.

   c.

8. List the four major types of economic systems. For each system, identify the method of resource allocation and how resources are owned.

    a.

    b.

    c.

    d.

SKILLS AND TOOLS

For each of the following items, follow the instructions, write the correct answer in the blank, or circle the correct answer.

1. By using its existing resources efficiently, an island society can produce the following alternative combinations of mangoes and oranges each day.

	Daily Production of:	
	Mangoes	**Oranges**
A	0	50
B	5	49
C	10	46
D	15	40
E	20	30
F	25	0

Oranges

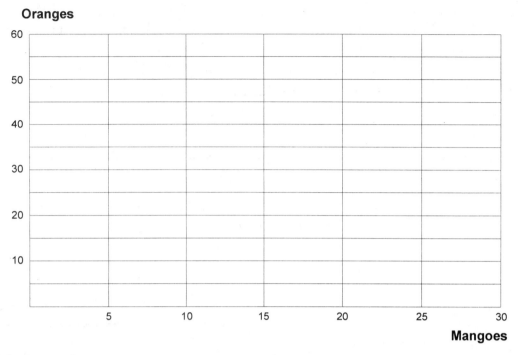

Mangoes

a. Plot this society's production possibility frontier (PPF) on the axes provided. Label the points A–F on your graph.

b. Assume the islanders are currently producing at point A, devoting all their resources to orange production. In moving to point B, this society gives up _____ orange(s). The resources released from producing oranges are then able to produce _____ mangoes. The opportunity cost to society of these first _____ mangoes is _____ orange(s).

Starting at point B, this society can move to point C and produce an additional _____ mangoes only if it foregoes an additional _____ oranges. The opportunity cost of the additional mangoes obtained in moving from B to C is an additional _____ oranges foregone.

In moving from C to D, the opportunity cost of _____ additional mangoes is _____ more oranges. In moving from D to E, the opportunity cost of _____ more mangoes is _____ more oranges. In moving from E to F, the opportunity cost of _____ more mangoes is _____ more oranges.

Moving along the PPF from A to F, the opportunity cost of mangoes is (increasing/ decreasing/constant) as more and more mangoes are produced.

   c. Now assume the islanders are currently producing at point F, devoting all their resources to mango production. In moving to point E, this society gives up

    _____ mangoes. The resources released from producing these

    mangoes are then able to produce _____ oranges. The opportunity

    cost to society of these first _____ oranges is _____

    mangoes.

    Starting at point E, this society can move to point D and produce an additional

    _____ oranges only if it foregoes an additional

    _____ mangoes. The opportunity cost of the additional oranges

    obtained in moving from E to D is an additional _____ mangoes

    foregone.

    In moving from D to C, the opportunity cost of _____ additional

    oranges is _____ more mangoes. In moving from C to B, the

    opportunity cost of _____ more oranges is _____

    more mangoes.

    Moving along the PPF from F to A, the opportunity cost of oranges is (increasing/ decreasing/constant) as more and more oranges are produced.

2. On the PPF above, plot the point representing total production of 10 mangoes and 30 oranges. Label this point G. Plot the point representing production of 15 mangoes and 50 oranges. Label this point H.

   a. At point G, the islanders (are/are not) using all their resources efficiently. Starting from point G, the opportunity cost of an additional 5 mangoes would be

    _____ oranges. The opportunity cost of an additional 5 oranges would

    be _____ mangoes. At point G, does this society achieve technical

    efficiency (yes/no)?

   b. The point H represents a combination of mango and orange production that this society (can/cannot) achieve with existing resources. To achieve point H, the technology of production will have to (improve/decline/remain the same) or society will have to (acquire more/use less) resources.

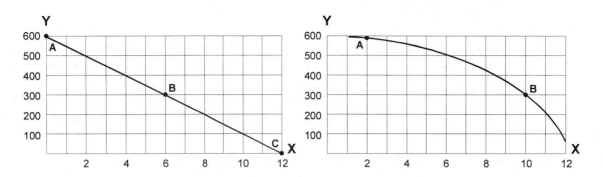

3. In the panel on the left above, the absolute value of the PPF's slope is (constant/increasing/decreasing) as we move from A to B. Starting at A, the opportunity cost of the first unit of good X will be _____ units of (X/Y). Starting at B, the opportunity cost of one more unit of X will be _____ units of (X/Y). If we begin at point C, the opportunity cost of one more unit of X will be _____ units of (X/Y). With this PPF, as we move from A to B to C, the opportunity cost of additional units of X is (constant/increasing/decreasing).

4. In the panel on the right above, as we move from point A to point B, the absolute value of the PPF's slope (remains constant/increases/decreases). At point A, the opportunity cost of an additional unit of X is (the same as/greater than/less than) the opportunity cost of an additional unit of X at point B. At the same time, at point A the opportunity cost of an additional unit of Y is (the same as/greater than/less than) the opportunity cost of an additional unit of Y at point B.

5. Each entry in the following table gives the number of hours it takes a typical worker in the given country to produce one unit of the indicated good. Thus, it takes a worker in Norway two hours to produce one sweater, and four hours to catch a fish, and so forth.

	Sweaters	**Fish**
Norway	2 hours	4 hours
Sweden	6 hours	2 hours

a. From these data, we can see that Norway has an absolute advantage in producing (sweaters/fish/both goods/neither good). At the same time, Sweden has an absolute advantage in producing (sweaters/fish/both goods/neither good).

b. From these same data, we can see that the opportunity cost of producing a fish in Norway is _____ sweater(s). The opportunity cost of producing a fish in Sweden is _____ sweater(s). From this we can conclude that Sweden has a comparative advantage in producing (sweaters/fish/both goods/neither good), while Norway has a comparative advantage in producing (sweaters/fish/both goods/neither good).

15-MINUTE PRACTICE TEST

Set a timer, giving yourself just 15 minutes to answer all of the following questions. To see what you *really* know and remember, take the test at least a day *after* you've read the chapter in the text and completed the exercises in this study guide.

Multiple Choice: Circle the letter in front of the single best answer.

1. The opportunity cost of any choice is
   a. the money given up for that choice.
   b. the time given up for that choice.
   c. what is actually sacrificed to make that choice.
   d. how much you would pay to make that choice.
   e. how much you would pay to avoid that choice.

2. For society, opportunity cost arises because of a scarcity of
   a. technology.
   b. land.
   c. money.
   d. resources.
   e. markets.

3. As we move rightward along a production possibilities frontier, we also move
   a. downward, and the frontier becomes steeper.
   b. downward, and the frontier becomes flatter.
   c. upward, and the frontier becomes steeper.
   d. upward, and the frontier becomes flatter.
   e. neither upward nor downward, and the slope of the frontier remains unchanged.

4. A point inside a production possibilities frontier might represent
   a. productive efficiency.
   b. a recession.
   c. a situation of very high opportunity cost.
   d. full employment of resources.
   e. none of the above.

5. The production possibilities frontier is concave shaped (like an upside-down bowl) because of
   a. the scarcity of resources.
   b. the law of increasing opportunity cost.
   c. productive inefficiency.
   d. absolute advantage.
   e. none of the above.

6. Which of the following is consistent with specialization according to comparative advantage?

    a. Famous attorney Alan Dershowitz prepares and addresses his own bills and takes them to the post office each day.

    b. John Travolta walks his own dog.

    c. The President of the United States drafts his own speeches.

    d. All of the above.

    e. None of the above.

7. One reason why specialization and exchange lead to greater production is

    a. comparative advantage.

    b. the development of expertise.

    c. the time saving from not having to switch tasks.

    d. all of the above.

    e. none of the above.

8. Which of the following is a method of resource allocation?

    a. Capitalism

    b. Socialism

    c. Command

    d. All of the above

    e. None of the above

9. Resource allocation involves an answer to which of the following questions?

    a. How are the economy's goods and services produced?

    b. What determines the rate of unemployment?

    c. How can business firms increase their profit?

    d. All of the above.

    e. None of the above.

10. Under *market capitalism*, resources are

    a. owned by society as a whole.

    b. owned by the market itself.

    c. owned by no one.

    d. allocated in an entirely random way.

    e. none of the above.

True/False: For each of the following statements, circle T if the statement is true or F if the statement is False.

T ~~F~~ 1. The correct measure of the cost of a choice is the time used up by that choice.

T ~~F~~ 2. The law of increasing opportunity cost tells us that the opportunity costs of our choices tend to rise over time.

T F 3. If we can produce more of one good without producing less of any other goods, the economy is productively inefficient.

T F 4. An individual has a comparative advantage in producing a good if he or she can produce it at a lower opportunity cost than some other individual.

T ~~F~~ 5. The United States is an example of a pure market economy, in which all resource allocation is accomplished through the market.

T F 6. An economic system is comprised of two components: a system of resource allocation and a system of resource ownership.

T ~~F~~ 7. A recession can be illustrated by a movement downward and rightward along a country's production possibilities frontier.

T ~~F~~ 8. The economic system of the former Soviet Union was market socialism.

CHAPTER 3

SUPPLY AND DEMAND

SPEAKING ECONOMICS

Fill in the blank with the appropriate word or phrase from the list provided in the word bank. (For a challenge, fill in as many blanks as you can *without* using the word bank.)

Aggregation
1. The process of combining distinct things into a single whole.

Imperfect Comp. Market
2. A market in which a single buyer or seller has the power to influence the price of the product.

Perfect Comp Market
3. A market in which *no* buyer or seller has the power to influence the price of the product.

IND. Q^D
4. The total amount of a good an individual would choose to purchase at a given price.

MARKET Q^D
5. The total amount of a good that buyers in a market would choose to purchase at a given price.

LAW OF D
6. "As the price of a good increases, the quantity demanded decreases."

D SCHEDULE
7. A list showing the quantities of a good that consumers would choose to purchase at different prices, with all other variables held constant.

D CURVE
8. A line showing the quantity of a good or service demanded at various prices, with all other variables held constant.

ΔQ^D
9. A movement along a demand curve in response to a change in price.

ΔD
10. A shift of a demand curve in response to a change in some variable other than price.

Income
11. The amount that a person or firm earns over a particular period.

wealth
12. The total value of everything a person or firm owns at a point in time, minus the total value of everything owed.

norm good   13. A good that people demand more of as their incomes rise.

infer good   14. A good that people demand less of as their incomes rise.

~~alternate good~~ SUBSTITUTE   15. A good that can be used in place of some other good and that fulfills more or less the same purpose.

complement   16. A good that is used together with some other good.

tech.   17. The set of methods a firm can use to turn inputs into outputs.

firm's quantity s   18. The amount of a good or service an individual firm would choose to produce and sell at a given price.

market Qs   19. The total amount of a good or service that sellers in a market would choose to produce and sell at a given price.

law of supply   20. "As the price of a good increases, the quantity supplied increases."

Supply Sced   21. A list showing the quantities of a good or service that firms would choose to produce and sell at different prices, with all other variables held constant.

SUPPLY CURVE   22. A line showing the quantity of a good or service supplied at various prices, with all other variables held constant.

$\Delta Q s$ 23. A movement along a supply curve in response to a change in price.

ΔS 24. A shift of a supply curve in response to some variable other than price.

Alternate good   25. Another good that a firm could produce using some of the same inputs as the good in question.

equilibrium   26. A situation that, once achieved, will not change unless some external factor, previously held constant, changes.

excess D   27. At a given price, the excess of quantity demanded over quantity supplied.

Excess S   28. At a given price, the excess of quantity supplied over quantity demanded.

Word Bank

aggregation
alternate good
change in demand
change in quantity demanded
change in quantity supplied
change in supply
complement
(market) demand curve
demand schedule
equilibrium
excess demand
excess supply
firm's quantity supplied
imperfectly competitive market

income
individual's quantity demanded
inferior good
law of demand
law of supply
normal good
perfectly competitive market
market quantity demanded
market quantity supplied
substitute
supply curve
supply schedule
technology
wealth

CHAPTER HIGHLIGHTS

Fill in the blanks with the appropriate words or phrases. If you have difficulty, review the chapter and then try again.

1. A _MARKET_ is a group of buyers and sellers with the potential to trade.

2. In defining a market, we must choose the geographic area in which _BUYERS_ and _SELLERS_ are located. The geographic area we choose depends on the specific question we are trying to answer.

3. In _IMP COMP._ markets, individual buyers and sellers have some influence over the price of the product.

4. In _PERFECT_ markets, each buyer and seller treats the _PRICE_ as given.

5. Supply and demand explain how prices are determined in _PERFECTLY COMPETITIVE_ markets.

6. The individual's quantity _DEMANDED_ of any good is the amount that an individual would choose to buy at a particular _PRICE_.

7. The ___market D___ of any good is the total amount that all buyers in a market would **choose** to purchase at a given ___P___.

8. The ___LAW___ of demand states that when the price of a good rises, and **everything else** remains the same, the quantity of the good demanded will ___↓___.

9. The ___D curve___ shows the relationship between the price of a good and the **quantity demanded,** holding constant all other variables that affect demand. Each point on **the curve** shows the quantity that buyers would choose to buy at a specific ___P___.

10. The law of demand tells us that demand curves slope ___downward___.

11. A change in a good's price causes us to *move along* the demand curve. We call this a change in ___QD___.

12. A change in any determinant of demand—except for the good's price—causes the demand curve to ___shift ___. We call this a ___ΔD___.

13. The demand for most goods (normal goods) is positively related to ___income___ or ___wealth___. A rise in either ___income___ or ___wealth___ will increase demand for these goods, and shift the demand curve to the ___right___.

14. When the price of a substitute rises, the demand for a good will ___↑___, shifting the demand curve to the ___right___.

15. A rise in the price of a complement will ___↓___ the demand for a good, shifting the demand curve to the ___left___.

16. A firm's ___tech___ is the set of methods it can use to turn ___Inputs___ into ___outputs___.

17. A competitive firm faces three constraints: (1) it's production technology, (2) the ___price___ of its inputs, and (3) the ___price___ of its output.

18. A firm's quantity ___supplied___ of any good is the amount it would choose to **produce and sell at a particular** ___P___.

19. The __M Q^S__ of any good is the total amount that sellers in a market would choose to produce and sell at a given price.

20. The *law of supply* states that when the price of a good rises, and everything else remains the same, the quantity of the good supplied will ___↑___.

21. The *supply curve* shows the relationship between the ___Q P___ of a good and the quantity supplied, holding constant the values of all other variables that affect supply. Each point on the curve shows the quantity that sellers would choose to sell at a specific ___P___.

22. The *law of supply* tells us that supply curves slope ___up___.

23. A change in a good's price causes us to *move along* the supply curve. We call this a change in ___Q S___.

24. A change in any influence on supply—except for the good's price—causes the supply curve to ___shift___. We call this a ___Δ S___.

25. A rise in the price of an input will cause supply to ___↓___, shifting the supply curve to the ___left___.

26. When an alternate good becomes more profitable to produce—because its price ___Q ↑___ or the cost of producing it ___↓___—the supply curve for the good in questions will shift to the ___left___.

27. Cost-saving technological advances cause supply to ___↑___, shifting the supply curve to the ___→___.

28. An increase in sellers' productive capacity shifts the supply curve to the ___→___.

29. A rise in the expected price of a good will ___↑ ↓___ the supply of the good, shifting the supply curve to the ___← ___.

30. A(n) ___equilib.___ is a situation that, once achieved, will not change unless something we have been holding constant changes.

31. To find the ___eq.___ price and quantity in a competitive market, draw the supply and demand curves. The ___intersect eq___ is the point where the two curves intersect.

32. Any change that shifts the supply curve to the _____←_____ will increase the equilibrium price and decrease the equilibrium quantity.

33. Any change that shifts the demand curve to the ___→___ will cause both the equilibrium price and quantity to increase

The next four problems concern the four key steps that economists use again and again to answer questions about the economy.

34. Key Step #1—Characterize the _____: Decide which _____ best suits the problem being analyzed, and identify the decision makers (buyers and sellers) who interact in that _____.

35. Key Step #2—Identify _____ and _____: Identify the _____ that the decision makers are trying to achieve, and the _____ they face in achieving those _____.

36. Key Step #3—Find the _____: Describe the conditions necessary for _____ in the market, and a method for determining that _____.

37. Key Step #4—What Happens when Things Change: Explore how events or government policies change the market _____.

IMPORTANT CONCEPTS

Write a brief answer for each of the following items.

1. List as many distinct variables as you can that *shift* the demand curve for a good. For each variable, indicate the direction of change that causes the demand curve to shift to the *left*. Assume that the good is *normal*.

    Income , wealth

    complement

    substitute , ø

    taste

2. List as many distinct variables as you can that *shift* the supply curve for a good. For each variable, indicate the direction of change that causes the supply curve to shift to the *right*.

In puts
alternate
~~tastes~~
tech
exp. price

3. What is the key difference between a perfectly competitive market and an imperfectly competitive market?

Indicate whether each of the next two statements is true or false, and then explain briefly.

4. "Income and wealth mean basically the same thing in economics."

F

5. "The phrase 'change in demand' can refer either to a shift in the demand curve or a movement along the demand curve."

F   ∂D shift
       ∂QD move along

SKILLS AND TOOLS

For each of the following items, follow the instructions, write the correct answer in the blank, or circle the correct answer.

1. In the following demand schedule, P is the market price and Q^D is the quantity of limousine rides demanded per week by buyers in Patterson, New Jersey.

DEMAND

P	Q^D
$100	0
80	4
60	8
40	12
20	16
0	20

Price
($ per ride)

a. Plot the market demand curve for limousine rides. Label this curve D.

b. From this demand curve, we can see that when the market price is $50, the quantity of limousine rides demanded will be _____ 10 _____. If the market price rises to $90, however, the quantity demanded will (rise/fall) to _____ 14 _____ units per week. However, if the market price falls as low as $10, the quantity demanded will (rise/fall) to _____ 2 _____ units per week.

2. In the following supply schedule, P is the market price of limousine rides and Q is the quantity of rides supplied per week by sellers in Patterson, New Jersey.

SUPPLY

P	Q^S
$ 20	0
40	4
60	8
80	12
100	16
120	20

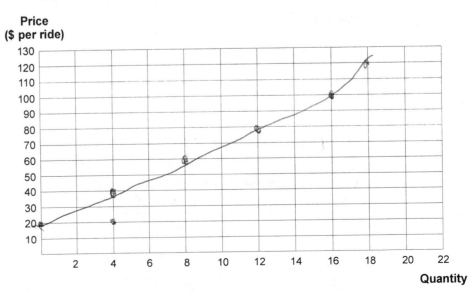

a. Plot the market supply curve for limousine rides in the space provided. Label this curve S.

b. From this supply curve, we can see that when the market price is $50, the quantity of rides supplied will be _____6_____ . If the market price rises to $90, however, the quantity supplied will (rise/fall) to _____14_____ units per week. However, if the market price falls as low as $30, the quantity supplied will (rise/fall) to _____2_____ units per week.

3. In the space below, re-plot the demand curve and the supply curve for limousine rides using the data from the previous two questions.

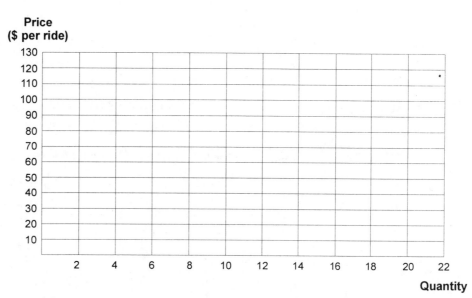

a. By examining demand and supply together, we can see that the equilibrium price in the market for limousine rides will be _____. The number of rides bought and sold per week will be _____.

b. At a price of $80 per week, there would be an excess (demand/supply) of _____ units per week in this market. Market price would tend to (rise/fall) as (buyers/sellers) compete with one another to (buy/sell) more limousine rides.

c. At a price of $40 per week, there would be an excess (demand/supply) of _____ units per week. Market price would tend to (rise/fall) as (buyers/sellers) compete with one another to (buy/sell) more limousine rides.

4. Under current conditions, the monthly demand curve and monthly supply curve for 13-inch color TVs in Golden, Colorado, are plotted below.

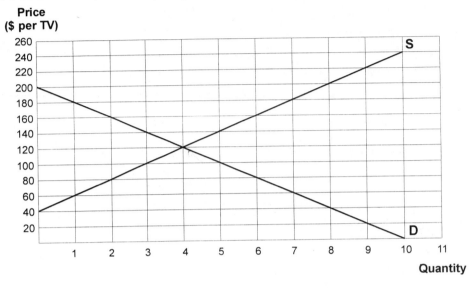

a. What is the equilibrium price of TVs? ___120___

b. Suppose the price of recliner chairs, a complement to TVs, falls. This will tend to (increase/decrease) the quantity of TVs demanded every month, and so shift market demand for TVs (rightward/leftward).

The table below shows data on market demand for TVs *after* the price of recliners has fallen.

P	Q^D
$200	2
160	4
120	6
80	8
40	10

c. Plot the new demand curve for TVs on the graph above.

d. What is the new equilibrium price for TVs? _____

e. Suppose the price of copper wire, an important component in the production of TVs, rises. This will tend to (increase/decrease) the quantity of TVs supplied every month, and so shift market supply of TVs (leftward/rightward).

Data on market supply of TVs after the price of copper wire has fallen are recorded in the table below.

P	Q^S
$120	2
160	4
200	6
240	8
280	10

f. Plot the new supply curve for TVs on the graph on the previous page.

g. What is the new equilibrium price for TVs after this latest change?

_____

5. Monthly data from Tuscaloosa on market demand and market supply of leather handbags have been graphed below.

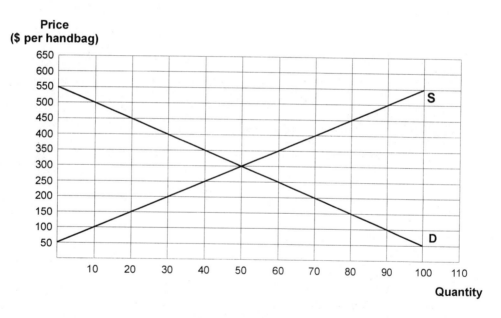

a. Complete the combined demand and supply schedules for leather handbags.

P	Q^D	Q^S
$450	_____	_____
400	_____	_____
350	_____	_____
300	_____	_____
250	_____	_____
200	_____	_____
50	_____	_____

b. If the market price were $400, quantity (demanded/supplied) would exceed quantity (demanded/supplied) and there would be an (excess demand/excess supply) equal to _____ units per period. This would cause the market price to (rise/fall) toward its equilibrium level of _____.

c. If the market price were $150, quantity (demanded/supplied) would exceed quantity (demanded/supplied) and there would be (excess demand/excess supply) equal to _____ units per period. This would cause the market price to (rise/fall) toward its equilibrium level of _____.

6. So far, we have studied market demand and market supply either as tables or as graphs. Sometimes, however, it is more convenient to express those same relationships in the form of equations. For example, suppose we know that, every week, the quantity of deep sea fishing trips buyers will demand (Q^D) is related to market price according to the equation

$$Q^D = 20 - P/15,$$

while the quantity of fishing trips supplied (Q^S) is related to market price according to the equation

$$Q^S = P/12 - 2.5.$$

Using these equations, complete the combined demand and supply schedules below. (To fill out the table, just plug market price into the demand or supply equation given above and solve for the corresponding quantity demanded or supplied.)

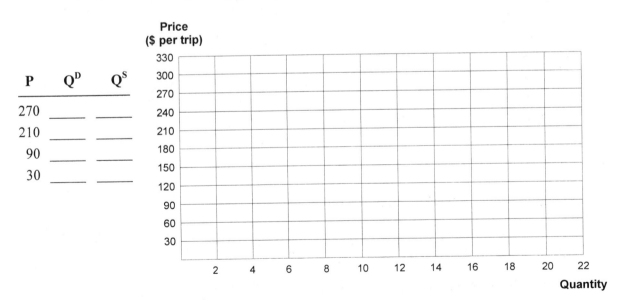

P	Q^D	Q^S
270	_____	_____
210	_____	_____
90	_____	_____
30	_____	_____

Now look at the table you just completed. Notice that at very low market prices, quantity demanded exceeds quantity supplied, while at higher prices quantity supplied exceeds quantity demanded. Just by looking at the data in these demand and supply schedules, we are therefore unable to determine the equilibrium price in this market.

But we *can* find the equilibrium with our equations. Suppose we let P_e stand for the unknown value of the equilibrium price in this market. While we do not know P_e, we know it is special: it is the only price at which quantity demanded will equal quantity supplied. To find P_e, we therefore simply set the equation for quantity demanded equal to the equation for quantity supplied. Setting $Q^D = Q^S$ in this way, we obtain

$$20 - P_e/15 = P_e/12 - 2.5.$$

To solve for P_e, we add 2.5 to each side, then add $P_e/15$ to each side, and get

$$22.5 = P_e/12 + P_e/15.$$

Next, putting the two terms on the righthand side over the common denominator $12 \times 15 = 180$, we obtain

$$22.5 = 27P_e/180.$$

Finally, by multiplying both sides by 180 and dividing by 27, we get the final answer

$$P_e = (22.5)(180)/27 = 150.$$

7. Using the data you generated in the preceding exercise, plot the market demand and supply curves in the space provided there. Once you've completed your graphs, locate the equilibrium market price. What is that price according to your graphs? _____ Is it the same price you obtained by solving the demand and supply equations? _____ It should be, so if it is not, go back and see what you did wrong.) What is the equilibrium quantity? _____ Is it the same as you would get if you plugged your answer for equilibrium price into the market demand and market supply curves? _____ (It should be.)

8. Annual market demand and market supply for tons of California cumquats are given, respectively, by the following equations

$$Q^D = 500 - P/8$$

$$Q^S = P/2 - 500.$$

Without plotting graphs for demand or supply, answer the following questions.

a. In equilibrium, the price of California cumquats will be $_____. The quantity of cumquats bought and sold will be _____ tons.

b. If market price were $1,200, quantity demanded would be _____ tons and quantity supplied would be _____ tons. There would be (excess demand/excess supply) equal to _____ tons of cumquats per year.

c. If market price were $2,000, quantity demanded would be _____ tons and quantity supplied would be _____ tons. There would be (excess demand/excess supply) equal to _____ tons of cumquats per year.

15-MINUTE PRACTICE TEST

Set a timer, giving yourself just 15 minutes to answer all of the following questions. To see what you *really* know and remember, take the test at least a day *after* you've read the chapter in the text and completed the exercises in this study guide.

Multiple Choice: Circle the letter in front of the single best answer.

1. In economics, a "market" is
    a. a geographic location where buyers and sellers trade with each other.
    b. virtually always defined locally, rather than nationally or internationally.
    c. virtually always defined nationally, rather than locally or internationally.
    d. defined only *after* an exchange actually takes place.
    e. a group of buyers and sellers with the potential to trade.

2. A perfectly competitive market is one in which
    a. buyers and sellers never actually meet each other.
    b. no buyer or seller can influence the price of the product being traded.
    c. a few very large firms directly compete with each other for customers.
    d. there are no limits to the tricks sellers can play to drive their rivals out of business.
    e. all of the above.

3. Which of the following would cause a rightward shift of the demand curve in the market for eggs in St. Louis?
    a. A technological advance in the egg-producing industry
    b. An increase in the number of firms in the egg-producing industry
    c. An increase in the price of chicken feed
    d. An increase in the price of powdered eggs, a substitute for fresh eggs
    e. None of the above

4. If used books are an inferior good, then a decrease in income will cause a
    a. rightward shift of the demand curve for used books.
    b. leftward shift of the demand curve for used books.
    c. rightward shift of the supply curve for used books.
    d. leftward shift of the demand curve for used books.
    e. shift in both the demand and the supply curves for used books.

5. If the price of oranges is expected to rise, then
   a. the demand curve for oranges will shift rightward.
   b. the demand curve for oranges will shift leftward.
   c. the supply curve for oranges will shift leftward.
   d. both *a* and *c*.
   e. both *b* and *c*.

6. Which of the following would shift the supply curve for a good leftward?
   a. A rise in the price of a complement
   b. A rise in the price of an input used in producing the good
   c. A cost-saving technological advance in producing the good
   d. All of the above
   e. None of the above

7. If there is an excess supply of a good, we can generally expect
   a. the price of the good to rise.
   b. the price of the good to fall.
   c. the demand curve to shift rightward.
   d. the supply curve to shift leftward.
   e. both *c* and *d*.

8. A rise in the price of a substitute for a good will cause
   a. the equilibrium price of the good to increase and the equilibrium quantity to decrease.
   b. the equilibrium price of the good to decrease and the equilibrium quantity to increase.
   c. both the equilibrium price and the equilibrium quantity of the good to increase.
   d. both the equilibrium price and the equilibrium quantity of the good to decrease.
   e. no change in either the equilibrium price or equilibrium quantity of the good.

9. Which of the following is *not* included among the four key steps that economists use to solve problems?
   a. Identify Goals and Constraints.
   b. Graph the Equations.
   c. Find the Equilibrium.
   d. What Happens when Things Change.
   e. Characterize the Market.

10. In the market for potatoes, a rise in the price of beef (a complement) and a rise in the wage paid to farm labor (an input) would cause
    a. both the equilibrium price and equilibrium quantity to rise.
    b. both the equilibrium price and equilibrium quantity to fall.
    c. a decrease in the equilibrium quantity, and an ambiguous effect on the equilibrium price.
    d. an increase in the equilibrium price, and an ambiguous effect on the equilibrium quantity.
    e. none of the above.

True/False: For each of the following statements, circle T if the statement is true or F if the statement is false.

T (F) 1. The law of demand tells us that, for most goods, a rise in income will cause an increase in quantity demanded.

T   2. If people want to buy more of a good at any price, sellers will want to sell more of the good, so the supply curve will shift.

T   F   3. A change in the expected future price of a good will cause both the supply curve and the demand curve for the good to shift.

T (F) 4. A "change in supply" refers to a movement along the supply curve.

(T) F   5. A rightward shift in the demand curve for cotton shirts will cause a rise in both the equilibrium price and equilibrium quantity of cotton shirts.

(T) F   6. A rise in the price of *rayon* shirts will cause a decrease in the equilibrium price and quantity of *cotton* shirts.

T (F) 7. The *first* key step of the four-step procedure is: Find the Equilibrium.

(T) F   8. The *last* key step of the four-step procedure is to ask: What Happens When Things Change?

CHAPTER 4

WHAT MACROECONOMICS TRIES TO EXPLAIN

Fill in each blank with the appropriate word or phrase from the list provided in the word bank. (For a challenge, fill in as many blanks as you can *without* using the word bank.)

Bus cycle   1. Fluctuations in real GDP around its long-term growth trend.

Expansion   2. A period of increasing real GDP.

Peak   3. The point at which real GDP reaches its highest level during a period of rising real GDP.

Recession   4. A period of declining real GDP.

trough   5. The point at which real GDP reaches its lowest level during a recession.

depression   6. An unusually severe recession.

Aggregation   7. The process of combining different things into a single category.

Word Bank

aggregation   peak
business cycles   recession
depression   trough
expansion

CHAPTER HIGHLIGHTS

Fill in the blanks with the appropriate words or phrases. If you have difficulty, review the chapter and then try again.

1. Economists—and society at large—agree on three important macroeconomic goals: rapid economic growth, full employment, and _____.

2. Economists monitor economic growth by keeping track of _____.

3. One measure economists use to keep track of employment is the _____.

4. In a typical business cycle, when output rises we are in the _____ phase, which continues until we reach a _____. Then, as output falls we enter a _____, and when output hits bottom, we are in a _____.

5. Macroeconomics makes extensive use of _____, the process of combining different things into a single category and treating them as a whole.

IMPORTANT CONCEPTS

Write a brief answer below each of the following items.

1. List the three important macroeconomic goals about which there is widespread agreement.

   a. *Rapid econ. growth*

   b. *Full Employment*

   c. *Stable prices*

2. What is the difference between an *expansion* and a *peak*?

   peak
   expan

3. What are the two types of disagreements that can arise on macroeconomics issues?

   a.

   b.

10-MINUTE PRACTICE TEST

Set a timer, giving yourself just ten minutes to answer all of the following questions. To see what you *really* know and remember, take the test at least a day *after* you've read the chapter in the text and completed the exercises in this study guide.

Multiple Choice: Circle the letter in front of the single best answer.

1. Which of the following is *not* a generally agreed-upon macroeconomic goal?
   a. Rapid economic growth
   b. High employment
   c. Low inflation
   d. Stable prices
   e. Zero unemployment

2. Which of the following is a *macro*economic question?
   a. Why do English professors generally earn less than business professors?
   b. Which automobile company makes the best product: General Motors, Ford, or Toyota?
   c. Why are apartment rents higher in San Francisco than in New York?
   d. Why, in the late 1990s, has real GDP in the United States been growing more rapidly than real GDP in England, France or Germany?
   e. Which nation has the best medical care: the United States, Canada, Germany, or England?

3. A recession is a period during which real GDP
   a. doesn't change.
   b. decreases.
   c. hits bottom.
   d. rises.
   e. reaches a peak.

4. A trough is a period during which real GDP
   a. doesn't change.
   b. falls.
   c. hits bottom.
   d. rises.
   e. reaches a peak.

5. A period of rising real GDP is called a(n)
   a. recession.
   b. inflation.
   c. peak.
   d. expansion.
   e. trough.

6. An inflation rate of zero means that the price level is
    a. falling, but very slowly.
    b. falling rapidly.
    c. not changing.
    d. rising, but slowly.
    e. rising rapidly.

7. In the United States, the goal of high employment
    a. is a good goal, but one that has never been written into law.
    b. is embodied in a law that calls for an unemployment rate of 4 percent.
    c. has virtually always been attained.
    d. has never been attained.
    e. is none of the above.

8. The British economist who originated modern macroeconomics by taking on the classical economists was named
    a. Milton Friedman.
    b. Robert Hall.
    c. John Maynard Keynes.
    d. Maynard G. Krebs.
    e. Sir Robert Denver.

True/False: For each of the following statements, circle T if the statement is true or F if the statement is false.

T F 1. When economists study output, employment, or inflation in small countries like Estonia or the Bahamas, they are practicing *micro*economics.

T F 2. In any period during which real GDP rises, output per person and the average standard of living automatically rise as well.

T F 3. The unemployment rate in the United States never reaches zero, even when the economy is doing well.

T F 4. The United States has never experienced double-digit inflation.

T F 5. While high unemployment is costly to society, high inflation is not.

CHAPTER 5

PRODUCTION, INCOME, AND EMPLOYMENT

SPEAKING ECONOMICS

Fill in each blank with the appropriate word or phrase from the list provided in the word bank. (For a challenge, fill in as many blanks as you can *without* using the word bank.)

GDP 1. The total value of all final goods and services produced for the marketplace during a given year, within the country's borders.

INTERMEDIATE GOOD 2. A good used up in producing a final good.

FINAL GOOD 3. A good sold to its final user.

FLOW VARIABLE 4. A measure of a process that takes place over a period of time.

STOCK ✓ 5. A measure of an amount that exists at a moment in time.

EXPENDITURE APPROACH 6. Measuring GDP by adding the value of goods and services purchased by each type of final user.

CONSUMPTION 7. The part of GDP purchased by households as final users.

CAPITAL STOCK ~~INVESTMENT PLANNING~~ 8. The total value of all goods that will provide useful services in future years.

PRIVATE INVESTMENT 9. The sum of business plant and equipment purchases, new home construction, and inventory changes.

NET INVESTMENT 10. Total investment spending minus depreciation.

GOV'T SPENDING 11. Spending by federal, state, and local governments on goods and services.

~~transfer payments~~ 12. Funds the government gives to people or organizations, but not as payment for goods or services.

Net EXPORTS 13. Total exports minus total imports.

Value added 14. The revenue a firm receives minus the cost of the intermediate goods it buys.

value added approach 15. Measuring GDP by summing revenue minus the cost of intermediate goods at all firms in the economy.

factor payments 16. Payments to the owners of resources that are used in production.

factor payments app. 17. Measuring GDP by summing the factor payments made by all firms in the economy.

nominal var. 18. A variable measured without adjusting for the dollar's changing value.

real var. 19. A variable adjusted for changes in the dollar's value.

nonmarket prod. 20. Goods and services that are produced, but not for sale in a market.

frictional 21. Joblessness experienced by people who are between jobs or who are just entering or reentering the labor market.

seasonal 22. Joblessness related to the time of year, such as job loss caused by changes in weather or tourist patterns.

structural 23. Joblessness arising from mismatches between workers' skills and employers' requirements or between workers' locations and employers' locations.

cyclical 24. Joblessness arising from changes in production over the business cycle.

F.E. 25. A situation in which there is no cyclical unemployment.

potential output 26. The level of output the economy could produce if operating at full employment.

labor force 27. Those people who have a job or who are looking for one.

unemployment Rate 28. The fraction of the labor force that is without a job.

involun pt. 29. Individuals who would like a full-time job, but who are working only part time.

discouraged workers 30. Individuals who would like a job, but have given up searching for one.

Word Bank

capital stock	labor force
consumption	net exports
cyclical unemployment	net investment
discouraged workers	nominal variable
expenditure approach	nonmarket production
factor payments	potential output
factor payments approach	private investment
final good	real variable
flow variable	seasonal unemployment
frictional unemployment	stock variable
full employment	structural unemployment
government purchases	transfer payments
gross domestic product (GDP)	unemployment rate
intermediate good	value added
involuntary part-time workers	value-added approach

CHAPTER HIGHLIGHTS

Fill in the blanks with the appropriate words or phrases. If you have difficulty, review the chapter and then try again.

1. The nation's _____GDP_____ (abbreviated GDP) is the total value of all _____final_____ goods and services produced for the marketplace during a given year, within _nation's borders_

2. To avoid overcounting __int.__ products when measuring GDP, we add up the value of _____final_____ goods and services only. The value of all _____int_____ products is automatically included in the value of the _____final_____ goods they are used to create.

3. Gross domestic product is a _____flow_____ variable: It measures a process—production—over a period of time.

4. In the _expenditure_ approach to measuring GDP, we add up the value of the final goods and services purchased by each type of final user.

5. Consumption is the part of GDP purchased by _households_ .

6. Private investment is the sum of (1) business purchases of _plant_ and _equip_ ; (2) new _home_ construction; and (3) changes in business firm's _inventories_ .

7. Total investment during the year is the sum of _____*Private*_____ investment and _____*gov't*_____ investment.

8. _____*Transfer*_____ payments represent money redistributed from one group of citizens (taxpayers) to another (the poor, the unemployed, the elderly). While _____*transfer*_____ are included in government budgets as spending, they are not payments for currently produced goods and services, and so are not included as part of government _____*purchase*_____ and not included in GDP.

9. To properly account for output sold to, and bought from, foreigners, we must include _____*Net*_____ exports—the difference between exports and _____*imports*_____.

10. A firm's value added is the revenue it receives for its output, minus the cost of all the _____*~~input~~ int. goods*_____ that it buys.

11. In the value-added approach, GDP is the sum of the values added by all _____*firms*_____ in the economy.

12. In any year, the value added by a firm is equal to the total _____*factor*_____ payments made by that firm.

13. In the factor payments approach, GDP can be measured by summing all of the factor payments made by all _____*firms*_____ in the economy. Equivalently, it can be measured by adding up all of the income—wages and salaries, rent, interst and _____*~~income~~ profit*_____ earned by all _____*households*_____ in the economy.

14. GDP—the total output of the economy—is equal to the total _____*income*_____ earned in the economy.

15. When a variable is measured over time with no adjustment for the dollar's changing value, it is called a _____*nominal*_____ variable. When a variable is adjusted for the dollar's changing value, it is called a _____*real*_____ variable.

16. Since our economic well-being depends, in large part, on the goods and services we can buy, it is important to translate _____*now*_____ values—which are measured in _____*current*_____ dollars—to real values—which are measured in _____*purchasing*_____ power.

17. ___*Short*___-term changes in real GDP are fairly accurate reflections of the state of the economy. A significant ___*Short*___-term drop in real GDP virtually always indicates a decrease in production, rather than a measurement problem.

18. In macroeconomics, full employment is achieved when ___*cyc.*___ unemployment has been reduced to zero. But the overall unemployment rate at full employment is greater than zero, because there are still positive levels of ___*seas*___, ___*struc.*___, and ___*fric*___ unemployment.

19. When there is cyclical unemployment, the nation *produces* less output, and so some group or groups within society must ___*consume*___ less output.

IMPORTANT CONCEPTS

Write a brief answer below each of the following items.

1. State the entire definition of gross domestic product. (Come as close as you can without looking at the text or the end-of-chapter answers.)

$$C + I + G + NX = GDP$$

2. What are the three different approaches to measuring GDP?

   a. FACTOR Payments

   b. Expenditure

   c. Value - Added

3. For each of the following transactions, state *yes* if it would be counted in the expenditure approach to GDP, and *no* if it would not. If *yes*, state which category of spending the transaction would contribute to (C, I, G or NX). If *no*, briefly state why not.

   a. _____G_____ Due to high crime in your area, your local police department hires two new police officers.

   b. _____No_____ You go to the ATM machine and withdraw $100 and put it in your wallet.

   c. _____No_____ A pick-pocket steals your wallet.

   d. _____C_____ You buy a new wallet at Macy's to replace the wallet the pick-pocket took.

   e. _____No_____ You sell your favorite videotape, *Terminator 12*, to a friend.

   f. _____I_____ You purchase a new computer to keep track of business at the poster store you own and manage.

   g. _____EX_____ Your poster store sells $1,000 worth of posters to a German retail poster outlet located in Berlin.

   h. _____I_____ During the year, your store's inventory of unsold posters increases by 100 posters.

4. Identify each of the following as either a *stock* variable or a *flow* variable.

   a. _____F_____ Your income

   b. _____F_____ The total income of everyone in the nation

   c. _____S_____ The funds in your bank account

   d. _____S_____ The value of your house

   e. _____S_____ The nation's capital stock

   f. _____F_____ Real GDP

   g. _____F_____ Investment spending

   h. _____F_____ Consumption spending

5. What are the four types of unemployment?

   cyc., struc, fric, seas

SKILLS AND TOOLS

For the following items, follow the directions, write the correct answer in the blank, or circle the correct answer.

1. Having applied for a job at the Commerce Department's Bureau of Economic Analysis, you are given the following hypothetical data to study before your interview. Figures are total value in billions of dollars.

Household spending on:

services	=	$3,008
nondurable goods	=	$1,776
durable goods	=	$706
Business spending on plant and equipment	=	$815 ✓
Wear and tear on factory equipment	=	$200
Inventory changes	=	$9 ✓
New homes constructed	=	$397 ✓
Existing homes which were destroyed	=	$123

State and Local Government spending on:

consumption	=	$540
investment	=	$113

Federal Government spending on:

consumption	=	$691
investment	=	$132
Depreciation of government assets	=	$245
Transfer payments	=	$2,936
Imports	=	$855
Exports	=	$961

You just *know* you're going to get some questions on this, so to get ready you ask yourself:

a. What is the total value of consumption spending in this economy?

_____5490_____

b. What is the total value of private investment spending in this economy?

_____1221_____

c. What is the total value of government purchases in this economy?

_____1476_____

d. What is the total value of net exports in this economy? _____106_____

e. Using the expenditure approach, what is GDP for this economy?

_8293_

f. Which entries in the table are not counted as part of the economy's GDP?

_____

2. The tiny island nation of Kuruma has two types of final goods: cars and food. Rubber is the only material used in making tires, and tires and steel are the only materials needed to make cars. Consumers buy cars from the dealer, who buys them from the manufacturer. Food in Kuruma is raised on farms and sold to consumers through supermarkets.

The government has collected firm-level data to help keep track of all this activity, but its information is incomplete. Here is what is has:

	Firm	Cost of Intermediate Goods	Revenue	Value Added
Cars	Rubber Company	$0	$0.75	.75
	Tire Company	.75	$1.50	.75
	Steel Company	$0	2.00	$2.00
	Car Manufacturer	3.50	$4.00	.50
	Car Dealer	4.00	4.50	$0.50
Food	Farmer	0	$0.75	$0.75
	Supermarket	.75	1.50	$0.25

a. Complete the table.

b. What is the GDP of Kuruma? _5.5_

3. There are only two firms in the economy of Gyroland: Summertime Farming (which makes sandwich ingredients) and Savory Sandwiches. Information on revenue and costs for these two firms is provided in the table.

Summertime Farming		**Savory Sandwiches**	
Total Revenue	$1,400	Total Revenue	$1,950
Costs		Costs	
wages to farmhands	$380	sandwich ingredients	$350
interest on loans	$115	wages to workers	$550
rent	$50	interest on loans	$200
		rent	$100

a. What is the total factor payment to labor in this economy? _930_

b. What is the total factor payment to capital in this economy? *315*

c. What is the total factor payment to land in this economy? *150*

d. What is the total profit in this economy? *1605*

e. Using the factor-payment approach, what is the GDP of Gyroland?

    3000

f. Explain briefly why GDP is *not* equal to the sum of total sales revenue at the two firms. (Hint: does all of this revenue result from the sale of *final* goods?)

4. The employment status of residents in a friendly country is given below. This country defines its terms and follows procedures established by the Bureau of Labor Statistics (BLS) in the United States.

Category	Population in millions
Under 16	55.0
Military	8.0
Institutionalized	4.0
Not in Labor Force	
Discouraged Workers	0.5
Full-time Students (age 16 and above)	33.0
All Others	30.0
Employed	
Involuntarily Part-time Workers	4.5
All Others	137.0
Unemployed	7.0

a. What is the size of the civilian noninstitutionalized population? *212*
    What is the size of the labor force? *148.5* What is the current
    unemployment rate? *.047   4.7%*

For each of parts (b) through (g), make all requested comparisons to the situation described in the preceding table.

b. If there is a baby boom and the number of individuals under 16 increases by 15 million, the size of the labor force will (increase/remain unchanged/decrease). The size of the labor force will then be *148.5* .

c. If full-time college students are drafted into the military, the size of the labor force will (increase/remain unchanged/decrease). The unemployment rate will (increase/remain unchanged/decrease).

d. If the number of unemployed individuals decreases by two million and the number of discouraged workers increases by two million, the size of the labor force will (increase/remain unchanged/decrease). The unemployment rate will (increase/remain unchanged/decrease) and will be ____3, 4____.

e. If three million unemployed individuals decide to stop looking for work, the size of the labor force will (increase/remain unchanged/decrease). The unemployment rate will (increase/remain unchanged/decrease) and will be ____2, 7____.

f. If seven million unemployed individuals find part-time employment, but really want full-time employment, the number of unemployed individuals will (increase/remain unchanged/decrease) and the unemployment rate will be ____0____.

g. If cuts in defense spending force two million military personnel out of the army to look for work, the size of the labor force will (increase/remain unchanged/ decrease). If the two million former military personnel are unable to find work, the unemployment rate will (increase/remain unchanged/decrease) and will be ____5.9____.

15-MINUTE PRACTICE TEST

Set a timer, giving yourself just 15 minutes to answer all of the following questions. To see what you *really* know and remember, take the test at least a day *after* you've read the chapter in the text and completed the exercises in this study guide.

Multiple Choice: Circle the letter in front of the single, best answer.

1. Fill in the blank: GDP is the total value of _____ produced for the marketplace during a given year, within the nation's borders.
    a. all goods
    b. all goods and services
    c. all final goods
    d. all final goods and services
    e. all final and intermediate goods and services

2. Which of the following is a flow variable?
    a. GDP
    b. Income
    c. Investment spending
    d. All of the above
    e. None of the above

3. Which of the following would be considered "private investment" in GDP?
    a. A computer printer purchased by a student
    b. A computer printer purchased by a law firm
    c. A computer printer purchased by the St. Louis police department
    d. All of the above
    e. None of the above

4. Net investment is equal to
    a. private investment.
    b. private investment plus government investment.
    c. private investment plus government investment minus depreciation.
    d. private investment plus government investment minus consumption spending.
    e. private investment minus government investment.

5. If Americans buy $500 billion worth of foreign goods and services, and foreigners buy $200 billion worth of American goods and services, then net exports for the United States are equal to
    a. −$700 billion.
    b. −$300 billion.
    c. $200 billion.
    d. $300 billion.
    e. $700 billion.

6. In the expenditure approach, GDP is equal to
    a. C + I + G.
    b. C + I + G + exports.
    c. C + I + G + imports.
    d. C + I + G + exports + imports.
    e. C + I + G + exports – imports.

7. When nominal GDP has increased in the United States, we know that
    a. U.S. output of goods and services has increased.
    b. the U.S. price level has increased.
    c. the U.S. price level has decreased.
    d. both U.S. output of goods and services *and* the price level have increased.
    e. either U.S. output of goods and services *or* the price level have increased.

8. One potential *problem* with the way GDP is measured is that it excludes
    a. nonmarket production.
    b. intermediate products.
    c. goods and services that are not sold during the year.
    d. all of the above.
    e. none of the above.

9. The economy is considered at "full employment" when
   a. the unemployment rate is zero.
   b. structural unemployment is zero.
   c. frictional unemployment is zero.
   d. cyclical unemployment is zero.
   e. none of the above.

10. The unemployment rate in the United States is defined as the number of unemployed divided by
    a. the U.S. population.
    b. the U.S. population over the age of 16.
    c. the number of employed.
    d. the number of employed minus the number of unemployed.
    e. the number of employed plus the number of unemployed.

True/False: For each of the following statements, circle T if the statement is true or F is the statement is false.

 T F 1. While short-term changes in real GDP can give a misleading picture of economic activity, long-term changes in real GDP give a fairly accurate picture.

 T F 2. U.S. GDP measures the production of goods and services by Americans, regardless of which country they reside in when they produce those goods and services.

T F 3. Goods that are not sold during the year are included as part of that year's investment in calculating GDP.

T F 4. When investment is greater than depreciation, net investment is positive and the capital stock grows.

T F 5. In the expenditure approach to GDP, government purchases include all spending on goods, services and transfer payments by government agencies.

T F 6. Structural unemployment is considered a *micro*economic problem.

 T F 7. Discouraged workers are people who used to work, but no longer want a job.

    T F 8. In the United States, one step in computing the unemployment rate is to count all those who apply for, and receive, unemployment insurance.

CHAPTER 6

THE MONETARY SYSTEM, PRICES, AND INFLATION

Fill in each blank with the appropriate word or phrase from the list provided in the word bank. (For a challenge, fill in as many blanks as you can *without* using the word bank.)

unit of value 1. A common unit for measuring how much something is worth.

means of payment 2. Anything acceptable as payment for goods and services.

Federal Reserve Bank 3. The central bank and national monetary authority of the United States.

Fiat Money 4. Anything that serves as a means of payment by government declaration.

price level 5. The average dollar price of goods and services in the economy.

index 6. A series of numbers used to track a variable's rise or fall over time.

CPI 7. A measure of the price level that tracks the cost of a fixed market basket of goods purchased by a typical household.

CPI inflation rate 8. The percentage change in the price level from one period to the next.

deflation 9. A falling price level.

indexing 10. Adjusting the value of some payment in proportion to a price index in order to keep the real payment unchanged.

nominal 11. A variable measured in current dollars.

real 12. A variable measured in terms of purchasing power.

GDP price index 13. A measure of the average price level of all final goods and services included in GDP.

nominal interest rate   14. The annual percent increase in a lender's dollars from making a loan.

real interest rate   15. The annual increase in a lender's purchasing power from making a loan.

Word Bank

Consumer Price Index
deflation
Federal Reserve System
fiat money
GDP price index
index
indexation
inflation rate

means of payment
nominal interest rate
nominal variable
price level
real interest rate
real variable
unit of value

CHAPTER HIGHLIGHTS

Fill in the blanks with the appropriate words or phrases. If you have difficulty, review the chapter and then try again.

1. When we measure change in the macroeconomy, we usually care not about the number of dollars we are counting, but the purchasing power those dollars represent. Thus, we translate _nominal_ values into real values, using the formula:

   real value = _nominal_ value/price index) × _100_

2. The _Consumer_ price index measures the prices of all goods and services that are included in U.S. GDP, while the _GDP_ price index measures the prices of all goods and services bought by U.S. households.

3. Inflation can redistribute purchasing power from one group to another, but it cannot, by itself, decrease the _avg_ real income in the economy.

4. Inflation can shift _purchasing power_ away from those who are awaiting future payments specified in dollars and toward those who are obligated to make such payments.

5. Over any period, the percentage change in a real value is approximately equal to the percentage change in the associated nominal value minus _inflation_ .

6. If inflation is fully _anticipated_ , and if both parties to a contract take it into account, then inflation will *not* redistribute purchasing power.

7. When inflationary expectations are ___*inaccurate*___ , purchasing power is shifted between those obliged to make future payments and those waiting to be paid. An inflation rate ___*higher*___ than expected harms those awaiting payment and benefits the payers; an inflation rate ___*lower*___ than expected harms the payers and benefits those awaiting payment.

8. When people must spend time and other ___*resources*___ coping with inflation, they pay an opportunity cost, that is, they sacrifice the goods and services those resources could have produced instead.

9. Although the BLS has partially fixed the problem, the CPI still suffers from substitutijon bias. That is, the CPI still overestimates the relative importance of the goods whose prices are rising ___*most rapidly*___ and underestimates the relative importance of goods whose prices are rising or rising ___*most slowly*___ . The result is an ___*over*___ -estimate of the inflation rate.

10. Because the CPI excludes many new products that lower the cost of living when they come on the market, it ___*overestimate*___ -estimates the inflation rate.

11. The CPI still fails to recognize that, in many cases, prices rise because of improvements in quality, not because the cost of living has risen. This causes the CPI to ___*overestimate*___ -estimate the inflation rate.

12. The CPI omits reductions in the prices people pay from more frequent shopping at discount stores, so the CPI ___*overestimates*___ -estimates the inflation rate.

13. When a payment is indexed, and the price index overstates inflation, inflation causes the real payment to ___*increase*___ , shifting purchasing power toward those who are indexed and away from the rest of society.

IMPORTANT CONCEPTS

Write a brief answer below each of the following items.

1. What is the key difference between *commodity* money and *fiat* money?

2. List two types of costs of inflation.

   a.

   b.

3. List three sources of bias in the CPI (your text discusses four). For each source of bias, state whether it causes the CPI to overestimate or underestimate the true rise in the price level.

   a. *Quality Changes*   *Overestimate*

   b. *new goods*   *over*

   c.

SKILLS AND TOOLS

1. The Weather Bureau recorded the daily temperature in Middletown, New York, and prepared the following table of monthly average temperature in degrees Fahrenheit.

	Average Temperature (Degrees F)	Temperature Index (May = 100)
January	33	_____
February	30	_____
March	42	_____
April	56	_____
May	70	_____
June	78	_____
July	84	_____
August	88	_____
September	79	_____
October	75	_____
November	63	_____
December	45	_____

   a. Compute a temperature index from the data in the table. Let the month of May be the base period; that is, construct your index so that it has a value of 100 for the month of May. Enter your index numbers in the in the blank column.

b. From May to June, the temperature index (increased/decreased) from

_____ to _____. From this we conclude that the

temperature in August was _____ percent (higher/lower) than it was in

May.

c. In November, the temperature index had a value of _____. This means

the temperature in November was _____ percent (higher/lower) than it

was in May.

d. Compared to the month of May, in what month(s) was the temperature approximately :

57% lower? _____

7% higher? _____

20% lower? _____

2. The Civil War had a dramatic impact on consumer prices in the United States. The table
below reports estimates of a price index like the CPI for the years 1855 through 1880.

Year	CPI (1860 = 100)
1855	104
1856	102
1857	105
1858	99
1859	100
1860	100
1861	106
1862	121
1863	151
1864	189
1865	196
1866	191
1867	178
1868	171
1869	164
1870	157
1871	147
1872	147
1873	144
1874	137
1875	132
1876	129
1877	129
1878	120
1879	120
1880	123

a. Plot the CPI from 1855 to 1880 on the grid provided.

b. Between 1860 and 1865, the CPI (increased/decreased) from _____ to
_____. By 1865 prices were _____ percent
(higher/lower) than they had been in 1860—a mere five years earlier. From 1865 to 1880,
prices (increased/decreased) rapidly. Nonetheless, by 1880, prices were still approximately
_____ percent (higher/lower) than they had been in 1860.

c. Copy the necessary CPI data from the table and compute the annual rate of inflation
between the indicated years to complete the table.

Remember: The inflation rate is the *percentage change* in the price level over the year. So,
for example, to compute the rate of inflation between 1863 and 1864, subtract the CPI in 1863
from the CPI in 1864, divide by the CPI in 1863, then multiply by 100.

Inflation Rate, 1863 to 1864

$$= \frac{CPI_{1864} - CPI_{1863}}{CPI_{1863}} \times 100$$

$$= \frac{189 - 151}{151} \times 100$$

$$= 25.2\%$$

Year	CPI	Inflation Rate	Year	CPI	Inflation Rate
1860	___		1865	___	
		___			___
1861	___		1866	___	
		___			___
1862	___		1867	___	
		___			___
1863	___		1868	___	
		25.2 %			___
1864	___		1869	___	
		___			___
1865	___		1870	___	

d. Between 1860 and 1865, the country experienced (inflation/deflation) in every year.
During those war years, the rate of (inflation/deflation) varied from a low of
_____ between the years _____ and
_____, to a high of _____ between the years
_____ and _____.

e. After the war, from 1865 to 1870, the country experienced (inflation/deflation) in every year. The country experienced the greatest rate of (inflation/deflation) between the years _____ and _____.

3. Nominal GDP, real GDP and the GDP price index in the United States are reported below. Nominal GDP is in billions of dollars. Real GDP is in billions of chained (1996) dollars.

Year	Nominal GDP	GDP Price Index	Real GDP
1989	5,489.1	83.3	6,591.8
1990	5,803.2	86.5	6,707.9
1991	5,986.2	89.7	6,676.4
1992	6,318.9	91.8	6,880.0
1993	6,642.3	94.0	7,062.6
1994	7,054.3	96.0	7,347.7
1995	7,400.5	98.1	7,543.8
1996	7,813.2	100.0	7,813.2
1997	8,300.8	101.9	8,144.8
1998	8,759.9	103.1	8,495.7
1999	9,256.1	104.6	8,848.2

a. Carefully examine nominal GDP and the GDP price index over the period 1989 to 1999. We can see from the table that nominal GDP (increased some years and decreased other years/increased every year/decreased every year) over the period. At the same time, the price level (increased some years and decreased other years/increased every year/ decreased every year).

b. On the grid below, plot nominal GDP and real GDP between 1989 and 1999. Be sure to label your graphs.

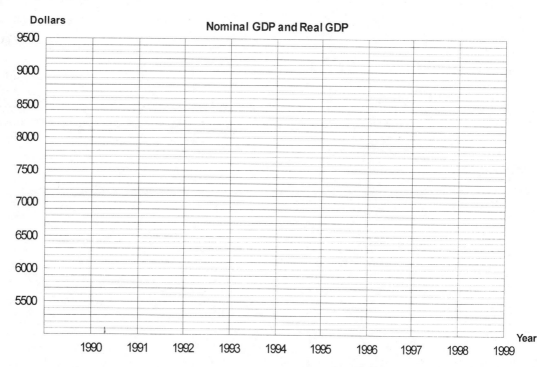

c. From a close examination of the table and graph, we can see that real GDP (did/did not) increase in every year over the period 1989 to 1999. From 1990 to 1991, real GDP (increased/decreased) from _____ to _____. Over the same period, nominal GDP (increased/decreased) from _____ to _____ and the price index (increased/decreased) from _____ to _____. Because real GDP (increased/decreased) while nominal GDP (increased/decreased) we can deduce that between 1990 and 1991 prices (increased/decreased) by a (greater/smaller) percentage than nominal GNP (increased/decreased).

4. The prime bank interest rate, commonly called the *prime rate*, is the interest rate banks charge their best and most credit-worthy customers. Data on the nominal prime, the real prime, and the rate of inflation are presented below.

Year	Prime Bank Interest Rate (Nominal)	Inflation Rate	Prime Bank Interest Rate (Real)
1989	_____	4.2%	6.7%
1990	10.0%	_____	5.7%
1991	8.5%	4.0%	_____
1992	6.3%	_____	3.5%
1993	_____	2.6%	3.4%
1994	7.1%	2.4%	_____
1995	8.8%	_____	6.2%
1996	8.3%	2.2%	_____
1997	_____	2.0%	6.4%
1998	_____	1.0%	7.4%
1999	8.0%	_____	6.5%

a. Complete the table.

b. Plot both the nominal prime rate and the real prime rate on the grid provided. Remember to label your graphs.

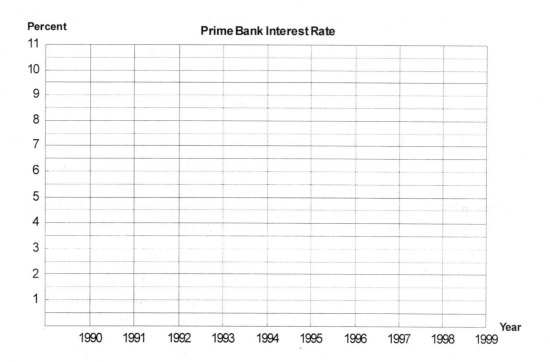

Percent   **Prime Bank Interest Rate**

15-MINUTE PRACTICE TEST

Set a timer, giving yourself just 15 minutes to answer all of the following questions. To see what you *really* know and remember, take the test at least a day *after* you've read the chapter in the text and completed the exercises in this study guide.

Multiple Choice: Circle the letter in front of the single best answer.

1. The paper currency that is now in use in the United States is an example of

    a. commodity money.
    b. fiat money.
    c. constitutional money.
    d. all of the above.
    e. none of the above.

2. The consumer price index tracks the average level of prices of all

    a. goods and services produced in the United States.
    b. final goods and services produced in the United States.
    c. final goods and services produced in the United States, plus imports into the United States.
    d. final goods and services produced by Americans, regardless of where they reside.
    e. goods and services purchased by consumers, whether they are produced in the United States or not.

3. Which of the following goods is *not* included in U.S. GDP, even though its price *is* included in the CPI?

    a. A new computer produced in the U.S. and purchased by an American household
    b. A new computer produced in the U.S. and purchased by an American corporation
    c. A second-hand computer purchased in the U.S. in a previous year, and now purchased by an American household
    d. A second-hand computer purchased in the U.S. in a previous year, and now purchased by a resident of Bulgaria.
    e. All of the above

4. Which of the following statements about inflation and the price level is true?

    a. When the price level is rising, the inflation rate must be rising as well.
    b. When the inflation rate is positive, the price level must be rising.
    c. When the inflation rate is falling, the price level can *not* be rising.
    d. When the inflation rate is zero, the price level must be zero as well.
    e. All of the above.

5. If your nominal wage rises from $5 to $7.50, while the price level rises from 100 to 150, then your real wage

    a. rises by 50%.
    b. rises by 25%.
    c. rises by 20%.
    d. does not change.
    e. falls.

6. If the nominal interest rate is 7 percent, and the annual inflation rate is 3 percent, then the real interest rate is

    a. −4%.
    b. −3%.
    c. 3%.
    d. 4%.
    e. 10%.

7. Inflation will redistribute purchasing power away from lenders and toward borrowers when

    a. the actual inflation rate turns out to be greater than expected.
    b. the actual inflation rate turns out to be smaller than expected.
    c. inflationary expectations are accurate.
    d. the inflation rate is higher than normal.
    e. the inflation rate is lower than normal.

8. Which of the following problems has caused the CPI to *overestimate* the rate of inflation?

    a. Substitution bias
    b. New technologies
    c. Quality changes
    d. All of the above
    e. None of the above

9. Which of the following is a change planned by the BLS to help eliminate the substitution bias of the CPI?
   a. A larger number of goods and services in the CPI
   b. A larger number of households in the CPI survey
   c. More frequent updates of the typical consumer's market basket
   d. Better estimates of the quality of goods and services
   e. None of the above

10. Which groups gain from the overstatement of inflation by the CPI?
   a. Workers with fixed nominal wages
   b. Recipients of social security payments
   c. Foreigners
   d. All Americans
   e. None of the above

True/False: For each of the following statements, circle T if the statement is true or F if the statement is false.

T   F   1. Over a period during which prices are rising, the inflation rate must be rising as well.

T   F   2. In the United States today, the dollar is accepted as payment for goods and services because the dollar is "backed" by the gold held in Fort Knox.

T   F   3. If the price index rises over the year from 200 to 230, then the rate of inflation for the year is 30%.

T   F   4. If your real wage is rising at the same time as the price level is rising, then your nominal wage must be rising as well.

T   F   5. When inflation is correctly anticipated, it is less likely to redistribute purchasing power between borrowers and lenders.

T   F   6. An example of the "resource cost" of inflation is when someone must re-tag a store's merchandise with new prices.

T   F   7. In the United States, the CPI is reported and calculated once each year.

T   F   8. In the United States, over the past twenty years, the CPI has risen about as often as it has fallen, and is now back pretty much where it started.

CHAPTER 7

THE CLASSICAL LONG-RUN MODEL

Fill in each blank with the appropriate word or phrase from the list provided in the word bank.
(For a challenge, fill in as many blanks as you can *without* using the word bank.)

Classical model   1. A macroeconomic model that explains the long-run behavior of the economy.

Mkt clearing   2. Adjustment of prices until quantities supplied and demanded are equal.

labor supply curve   3. Indicates how many people will want to work at various wage rates.

labor demand curve   4. Indicates how many workers firms will want to hire at various wage rates.

Agg. production fctn   5. The relationship showing how much total output can be produced with different quantities of labor, with land, capital, and technology held constant.

Circular flow   6. A diagram that shows how goods, resources, and dollar payments flow between households and firms.

Say's law   7. The idea that total spending will be sufficient to purchase the total output produced.

Net taxes   8. Government tax revenues minus transfer payments.

Saving   9. The portion of after-tax income that households do not spend on consumption goods.

leakages   10. Income earned, but not spent, by households during a given year.

injections
~~planned investment spending~~   11. Spending from sources other than households.

Planned investmnt spending   12. Business purchases of plant and equipment.

loanable funds mkt   13. A market in which households make their savings available to borrowers.

65

deficit _____ 14. The excess of government purchases over net taxes.

surplus _____ 15. The excess of net taxes over government purchases.

national debt _____ 16. The total amount that the federal government owes.

supply of funds curve 17. Indicates the level of household saving at various interest rates

investment demand curve 18. Indicates the level of investment spending firms plan at various interest rates.

govt demand for funds curve 19. Indicates the amount of government borrowing at various interest rates.

total demand for funds curve 20. Indicates the total amount of borrowing at various interest rates.

fiscal policy _____ 21. A change in government purchases or net taxes designed to change total spending and total output.

crowding out _____ 22. A decline in one sector's spending caused by an increase in some other sector's spending.

complete crowding out 23. A dollar-for-dollar decline in one sector's spending caused by an increase in some other sector's spending.

Word Bank

aggregate production function
budget deficit
budget surplus
circular flow
classical model
complete crowding out
crowding out
fiscal policy
government demand for funds curve
(household) saving
injections
investment demand curve

labor demand curve
labor supply curve
leakages
loanable funds market
market clearing
national debt
net taxes
planned investment spending
Say's law
supply of funds curve
total demand for funds curve

CHAPTER HIGHLIGHTS

Fill in the blanks with the appropriate words or phrases. If you have difficulty, review the chapter and then try again.

1. While Keynes's ideas and their further development help us understand economic fluctuations—movements in output around the long-run trend—the _classical_ model has proven more useful in explaining the long-run trend itself.

2. A critical assumption in the classical model is that _market clearing_: The price in every market will adjust until quantity supplied and quantity demanded are equal.

3. In order to earn income so we can buy goods and services, we must supply labor and other _services_ to firms.

4. The labor supply curve slopes _upward_ because—as the wage rate _increases_—more and more individuals are better off working than not working. Thus, a _decrease increase_ in the wage rate increases the number of people in the economy who want to work—to supply their labor.

5. As the wage rate _increases_, each firm in the economy will find that—to maximize profit—it should employ fewer workers than before. When all firms behave this way together, a _increase_ in the wage rate will decrease the quantity of labor demanded in the economy. This is why the economy's labor demand curve slopes _downward_.

6. In the _classical long run_ view, the economy achieves full employment on its own.

7. The aggregate production function shows the total output the economy can produce with different quantities of _labor_, holding constant the amounts of land and capital and the current state of _technology_.

8. In the classical, long-run view, the economy reaches its _potential_ output level automatically.

9. In a simple economy with just households and firms, in which households spend all of their income, total spending must be equal to total _output_.

10. _Say_'s law states that by producing goods and services, firms create a total demand for goods and services equal to what they have produced.

11. Total spending will equal total output if and only if total leakages in the economy are equal to total ___*injections*___; that is, only if the sum of saving and ___*taxes*___ is equal to the sum of investment spending and ___*gvt purchases*___ .

12. When government purchases of goods and services (G) are greater than net taxes (T), the government runs a budget ___*deficit*___ equal to ___$G-T$___ . When government purchases of goods and services (G) are less than net taxes (T), the government runs a budget ___*surplus*___ equal to ___$T-G$___ .

13. ___*Local*___ and ___*state*___ governments, like the federal government, can run deficits and surpluses, requiring them to participate in the loanable funds market. In our classical model, we aggregate all of these levels of government together and refer only to *the government*. When the government runs a budget ___*deficit*___ , it demands loanable funds equal to its ___*deficit*___ . When the government runs a budget ___*surplus*___ , it supplies loanable funds equal to its ___*surplus*___ .

14. The quantity of funds supplied to the financial market depends positively on the ___*interest*___ . This is why saving, or the supply of funds curve, slopes upward.

15. When the interest rate ___*falls*___ , investment spending and the business borrowing needed to finance it rise. The investment demand curve slopes ___*downward*___ .

16. The government sector's deficit and, therefore, its demand for funds are independent of the ___*int rate*___ .

17. As the interest rate decreases, the quantity of funds demanded by business firms ___*increase*___ , while the quantity demanded by the government ___*same*___ . Therefore, the total quantity of funds demanded ___*increase*___ .

18. As long as the ___*loanable funds*___ market clears, Say's law holds even in a more realistic economy with saving, taxes, investment, and a government deficit.

19. Fiscal policy is a change in ___*gvt*___ purchases or in ___*taxes*___ designed to change total spending in the economy and thereby influence the levels of employment and ___*output*___ .

20. Crowding out is a (an) ___*increase*___ in one sector's spending caused by a (an) ___*decrease*___ in some other sector's spending.

21. In the _____*non classical*_____ model, a rise in government purchases completely crowds
     out _____*private*_____ sector spending, so total spending remains unchanged.

22. If the government increases its purchases, it just removes funds from the
     _____*loanable funds*_____ market that would have been spent by _____*firms*_____ or
     by households. Thus, an increase in government purchases has no impact on total spending
     and no impact on total output or total employment.

IMPORTANT CONCEPTS

Write a brief answer below each of the following items.

1. What two words describe the key critical assumption in the classical model? Briefly, what
    does this assumption mean?

    markets clear

2. Which *two* graphs are necessary to determine the equilibrium level of output in the classical
    model?

    a. *LABOR*

    b. *Agg. Prod func.*

3. Which single graph is necessary to determine the equilibrium interest rate in the classical
    model?

    loanable funds.

4. List the two types of leakages and the two types of injections in the macroeconomy.

Leakages: a.   *savings*

                b. *taxes*

Injections: a.   *Ip*

                b. *Gov spending*

5. Suppose the government increases G, its purchases of goods and services. In the classical view, how is each of the following variables affected? In each case, write increase, decrease, no change, or ambiguous.

    a. real output _____∅_____—_____

    b. employment _____—_____

    c. interest rate _____∅ ↑_____

    d. (real) household saving _____∅ ↑_____

    e. (real) business investment _____∅ ↓_____

1. Classica's northern neighbor, Upper Classica, is a large economy. Labor supply depends on the real wage, and that relationship is graphed below. Labor demand depends on the real wage, too, and it is given by the equation

$$L^D = 192 - 4W$$

where W is the real hourly wage and L^D is millions of workers demanded.

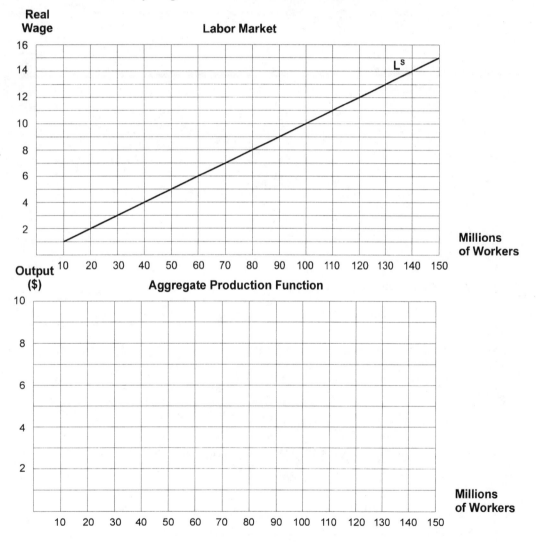

a. Graph Upper Classica's labor demand curve in the appropriate panel.

b. If the real wage in this economy were $12, firms would want to hire _____ million workers, while a total of _____ million workers would be willing to work. Because there is (excess demand/ equilibrium/excess supply) in the labor market at a wage of $12, wages will have a tendency to (rise above/remain at/fall below) $12 in this economy.

c. If the real wage in this economy were $8, firms would want to hire _____ million workers, while a total of _____ million workers would be willing to work. Because there is (excess demand/equilibrium/excess supply) in the labor market at a wage of $8, wages will have a tendency to (rise above/remain at/fall below) $8 in this economy.

d. If the real wage in this economy were $10, firms would want to hire _____ million workers, while a total of _____ million workers would be willing to work. Because there is (excess demand/ equilibrium/excess supply) in the labor market at a wage of $10, wages will have a tendency to (rise above/remain at/fall below) $10 in this economy.

e. Given the current state of its technology, and its stocks of capital and land, the aggregate production function in Upper Classica is

$$Y = \frac{\sqrt{L}}{2}$$

where Y is total real output (in trillions of dollars) and L is total employment. Plot this production function in the appropriate panel of the grid provided.

f. What is the full-employment output level in Upper Classica? _____

2. In the economy of Upper Classica, described in the previous problem, the supply of savings from households, S, depends on the interest rate according to the equation

$$S = \frac{r - 1}{2}.$$

where *r* is the interest rate measured in percentage points (e.g. seven percent is 7 rather than decimal 0.07).

The demand for funds arises from (1) the business sector's investment spending and (2) the government sector's budget deficit.

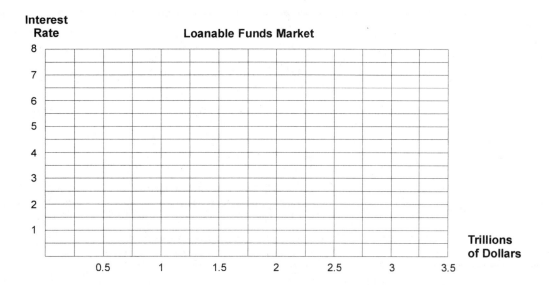

a. Plot the supply of funds curve on the grid provided. Label this curve *Supply*.

b. Businesses in Upper Classica are like business in most countries. As the interest rate falls, their planned investment spending (rises/falls/remains unchanged). To finance their investment spending, businesses (demand/supply) funds in the loanable funds market. In fact, business borrowing to finance investment in Upper Classica is given by the following equation:

$$I = 3.0 - (1/2)r.$$

Because the slope of this relationship is (negative/zero/positive), we can see that borrowing to finance investment spending will increase as the interest rate (decreases/remains unchanged/increases).

c. In Upper Classica, government purchases (G) are always $1.5 trillion. Net taxes (T) are $1.0 trillion. Because government purchases exceed net taxes, the government budget (surplus/deficit) will be _____ trillion dollars per year. We can write this as follows:

$$G - T = \text{_____} .$$

To finance this (surplus/deficit), the government will (demand/supply) funds in the loanable funds market. Specifically, the government will (lend/borrow) loanable funds in the amount of _____ trillion dollars, no matter what the interest rate may be.

d. To obtain the total demand for funds, we must (add/subtract) business firms' demand and the government's demand for funds. From the information in parts (b) and (c), we can determine that the total demand for funds in Upper Classica is given by the equation:

Total Demand for Funds = _____ .

Plot the total demand for funds on the grid provided, and label your graph *Demand*.

e. From the graph, we can see that if the interest rate in Upper Classica is 6%, there will be (excess demand/equilibrium/excess supply) in the loanable funds market. According to the classical model, we should expect the interest rate to (rise above/remain unchanged at/fall below) this level. If the interest rate is 3%, there will be (excess demand/equilibrium/excess supply) in the loanable funds market. We should then expect the interest rate to (rise above/remain unchanged at/fall below) this level. In Upper Classica, the loanable funds market will be in equilibrium when the interest rate is _____ percent.

f. When the interest rate is at its equilibrium level in the loanable funds market, the total demand for funds will be _____ trillion dollars. Of this, the government (surplus/deficit) will be the amount $G - T =$ _____, and investment demand will be $I^p =$ _____ trillion dollars. At this same interest rate, the total supply of funds will be _____ trillion dollars, and of this, household saving will be the amount $S =$ _____ trillion dollars.

g. Review the preceding parts of this problem, then complete the following table to describe the spending flows in Upper Classica. (Hint: Consumption must be what is left of total income after subtracting net taxes and household saving.)

Flows in the Economy of Upper Classica
(Trillions of Dollars)

Total Output	5.0
Total Income	_____
Consumption Spending (C)	_____
Investment Spending (I^p)	_____
Government Spending (G)	_____
Net Taxes (T)	_____
Household Saving (S)	_____

h. When, as in part (f), the total quantity of funds supplied equals the total quantity of funds demanded, leakages out of the income-spending stream will (exceed/equal/fall below) total injections. Total leakages, or the sum (S+T / I^P+G / I+T), amount to _____ trillion dollars in Upper Classica. Total injections, or the sum (S+T / I^P+G/ I^P+T), amount to _____ trillion dollars. Thus, at the interest rate that clears the loanable funds market, the economy of Upper Classica (does/does not) satisfy Say's Law.

3. Policy makers in Upper Classica are not satisfied with things the way they are. Some people have suggested that the government should increase its spending above its current level of $1.5 trillion. On the grid below, copy the demand and supply of funds curves you plotted in the previous problem. Then answer the following questions.

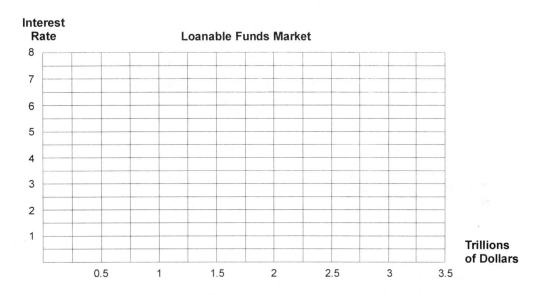

a. Suppose the government decides to increase its purchases by $1 trillion. This will cause the (demand curve/supply curve) for funds to shift (leftward/rightward) by an amount just equal to _____ trillion dollars at every level of the interest rate. With this in mind, plot the new (demand/supply) curve.

b. After the increase in government purchases, the equilibrium interest rate will (rise/fall) to _____ percent. This (increase/decrease) in the equilibrium interest rate will cause households to (increase/decrease) saving and to (increase/decrease) consumption spending. It will also cause investment spending by firms to (increase/decrease).

c. From a careful reading of the graph, we can see that the (increase/decrease) in the equilibrium interest rate causes household saving to (increase/decrease) by exactly _____ trillion dollars, and so causes consumption spending to (increase/decrease) by exactly

_____ trillion dollar(s). At the same time, investment spending by businesses (increases/decreases) by exactly _____ trillion dollar(s). From this we can see that the original $1 trillion increase in government spending caused spending elsewhere in the economy to (increase/decrease) by (a larger amount/the same amount/a smaller amount). Thus, the original increase in government spending (did/did not) result in complete crowding out.

15-MINUTE PRACTICE TEST

Set a timer, giving yourself just 15 minutes to answer all of the following questions. To see what you _really_ know and remember, take the test at least a day _after_ you've read the chapter in the text and completed the exercises in this study guide.

Multiple Choice: Circle the letter in front of the single best answer.

1. According to the classical view, which of the following statements is true?
   a. Fiscal policy cannot change real output or employment.
   b. Fiscal policy can change output but not employment.
   c. Fiscal policy can change employment but not output.
   d. All of the above.
   e. None of the above.

2. The key critical assumption in the classical model is that
   a. fiscal policy is ineffective.
   b. output and income are equal.
   c. the government is running a budget deficit.
   d. the budget deficit does not depend on the interest rate.
   e. markets clear.

3. Say's law tells us that
   a. markets clear.
   b. total spending is equal to total output.
   c. total income is equal to total output.
   d. the budget deficit is equal to household saving.
   e. investment spending is equal to household saving.

4. The government's budget deficit is equal to
   a. government purchases minus total taxes.
   b. government purchases plus total taxes.
   c. government purchases minus the difference between total taxes and transfer payments.
   d. government purchases minus transfer payments.
   e. government purchases plus investment spending minus total taxes.

5. Which of the following is a "leakage" in the macroeconomy?
   a. Household saving
   b. Consumption spending
   c. Investment spending
   d. Government spending
   e. None of the above

6. The total demand for funds curve slopes downward because a rise in the interest rate causes
   a. government borrowing to decrease.
   b. business borrowing to decrease.
   c. both government borrowing and business borrowing to decrease.
   d. household saving to increase.
   e. consumption spending to decrease.

7. When the government is running a budget deficit, the loanable funds market will clear when household saving plus net taxes is equal to
   a. investment spending plus the government's budget deficit.
   b. investment spending plus government purchases.
   c. consumption spending plus the budget deficit.
   d. consumption spending plus investment spending plus government spending.
   e. consumption spending

8. When the government is running a budget surplus, the loanable funds market will clear when household saving plus the budget surplus is equal to
   a. net taxes.
   b. investment spending.
   c. government purchases.
   d. investment spending plus government purchases.
   e. investment spending plus net taxes.

9. In the classical view, if government purchases rise (and there is no other fiscal change),
   a. employment.
   b. the interest rate rises.
   c. the real wage rises.
   d. output rises.
   e. all of the above.

10. According to the classical model, to ensure that the economy reaches its potential output level, the government
    a. must run a budget deficit.
    b. must run a budget surplus.
    c. must run a balanced budget.
    d. must set its purchases equal to private investment spending.
    e. need not worry about its fiscal policy.

True/False: For each of the following statements, circle T if the statement is true or F if the statement is false.

T   (F)   1. The classical model takes a short-run view of the economy, while the Keynesian model takes a more long-run view.

T   (F)   2. According to the classical view, the economy needs the government's help in achieving full employment.

T   (F)   3. The aggregate production function tells us how much output can be produced with different amounts of capital and land, and a fixed amount of labor.

(T)(F)   4. "Net taxes" are equal to the government's total tax revenue minus government transfer payments.

(T)(F)   5. Investment spending and government purchases play the role of "injections" in the macroeconomy.

(T)   F   6. In the classical model, an increase in government spending—with no other change—will shift the total demand for funds curve rightward.

T   (F)   7. The key conclusions of the classical model do not hold if the government is running a budget surplus rather than a budget deficit.

(T)   F   8. In the classical model, an increase in government purchases causes household saving to increase, and household consumption spending to decrease.

CHAPTER 8

ECONOMIC GROWTH AND RISING LIVING STANDARDS

Fill in each blank with the appropriate word or phrase from the list provided in the word bank.
(For a challenge, fill in as many blanks as you can *without* using the word bank.)

capital /per worker

productivity 1. Total output (real GDP) per person.

capital per person _productivity_ 2. Total output (real GDP) per worker.

avg standard of living 3. The total capital stock divided by total employment.

corporate profits tax 4. A tax on the profits earned by corporations.

corporate gains tax 5. A reduction in taxes for firms that invest in certain favored types of capital.

capital gains tax 6. A tax on profits earned when a financial asset is sold at more than its acquisition price.

consumption tax 7. A tax on the part of their incomes that households spend.

human capital 8. Skills and knowledge possessed by workers.

technological change 9. The invention or discovery of new inputs, new outputs, or new production methods.

patent protection 10. A government grant of exclusive rights to use or sell a new technology.

Word Bank

average standard of living

capital gains tax

capital per worker

consumption tax

corporate profits tax

human capital

investment tax credit

patent protection

productivity (or labor productivity)

technological change

CHAPTER HIGHLIGHTS

Fill in the blanks with the appropriate words or phrases. If you have difficulty, review the chapter and then try again.

1. Achieving a higher rate of growth in the _____long_____ run generally requires some sacrifice in the _____short_____ run.

2. When output grows faster than _____population_____, GDP per capita—which we call the average standard of living—will _____increase_____. When output grows more slowly than _____population_____, GDP per capita, or the average standard of living, will _____decrease_____.

3. Growth in employment can arise from an increase in labor supply (a _____right_____ shift in the labor supply curve) or an increase in the labor demand (a _____right_____ shift in the labor demand curve).

4. A cut in tax rates increases the reward for working, while a cut in benefits to the needy increases the hardship for not working. Either policy can cause a greater rightward shift in the economy's labor _____supply_____ curve than would otherwise occur and speed the growth in employment and output.

5. Government policies that help increase the skills of the workforce or that subsidize employment more directly shift the economy's labor _____supply_____ curve to the right, increasing employment and output.

6. When employment increases, while the capital stock remains constant, the amount of capital available to the average worker will _____fall_____, and labor productivity will _____fall_____.

7. If the capital stock grows faster than _____employment_____, then capital per worker will rise, and labor productivity will increase along with it. But if the capital stock grows more slowly than _____employment_____, then capital per worker will fall, and labor productivity will fall as well.

8. Reducing business _____corporate taxes_____ or providing specific investment incentives can shift the investment curve _____right_____, thereby speeding growth in physical capital, and increasing the growth rate of living standards.

9. Government can alter the tax and transfer system to increase incentives for _____saving_____. If successful, these policies would make more funds available for investment, speed growth in the capital stock, and speed the rise in living standards.

10. A shrinking budget deficit or a _growing_ budget surplus tends to _lower_ interest rates and _increase_ investment, thus speeding the growth in the capital stock.

11. Government investment in new capital and in the maintenance of existing capital makes an important contribution to economic growth. Thus, the impact of deficit reduction on economic growth depends on which government programs are cut. Shrinking the deficit by cutting government _investment_ will not stimulate growth as much as would cutting other types of government spending.

12. An increase in _human_ capital works much like an increase in physical capital to increase output: It causes the production function to shift _right_, raises productivity, and increases the average standard of living.

13. Many pro-growth policies—policies that increase employment or increase investment in physical capital—are also effective in promoting investment in _human_ capital.

14. The faster the rate of technological change, the greater the growth rate of productivity, and the faster the rise in living standards. The rate of technological change in an economy depends largely on firms' total spending on _the R & D_. Policies that increase _R & D_ spending will increase the pace of technological change.

15. Government policy is constrained by the reactions of private decision makers. As a result, policymakers face _trade offs_: Making progress toward one goal often requires some sacrifice of another goal.

16. Promoting economic growth involves unavoidable _trade offs_: It requires some groups, or the nation as a whole, to give up something else that is valued. In order to decide how fast we want our economy to grow, we must consider growth's _costs_ as well as its benefits.

17. Properly targeted tax _cuts_ can increase the rate of economic growth, but will force us to either redistribute the tax burden or cut government programs.

18. Greater investment in physical capital, human capital, and R&D will lead to faster economic growth and higher living standards in the future, but we will have fewer _consumption_ goods to enjoy in the present.

19. A (an) _increase_ in the fraction of the population with jobs or a (an) _increase_ in working hours will increase output and raise living standards, but also require us to sacrifice time previously spent in nonmarket activities.

20. We can achieve greater worker safety, a cleaner environment, and other social goals, but we may have to sacrifice some economic _____growth_____ along the way. Alternatively, we can achieve greater economic _____growth_____, but we will have to compromise on other things we care about.

21. In order to have rising living standards, a nation's stock of capital must not only grow, but grow faster than its _____population_____.

22. The poorest LDCs are too poor to take advantage of the trade-off between producing _____Capital_____ goods and producing _____consumption_____ goods in order to increase their living standards. Since they cannot tolerate a decrease in the production of _____Capital_____ goods below current levels, they cannot produce enough _____Consumption_____ goods to keep up with their rising populations.

IMPORTANT CONCEPTS

Write a brief answer below each of the following items.

1. Each of the different methods of promoting economic growth can be illustrated as a curve shift (or more-rapid-than-otherwise curve shift) in one of the three classical market diagrams: the labor market, the production function, or the loanable funds market. For each growth-promoting change listed below, state (1) which diagram would be most directly affected, (2) which curve shifts or shifts more rapidly as a result of the change; and (3) the direction of the shift. (You may want to draw diagrams to help with your answer.)

   a. an increase in population with no change in the labor force participation rate

   b. an increase in the labor force participation rate with no change in population

   c. a cut in the tax rate on wages

d. increased spending on educating and training the workforce

e. reduction in the corporate profits tax rate

f. reduction in the capital gains tax

g. decrease in the budget deficit

h. increase the budget surplus

i. more rapid technological change

2. List three different types of costs society may have to pay for faster economic growth (the text discusses four types of costs):

    a.

    b.

    c.

3. List three characteristics of many less-developed countries that help explain their low growth rates.

    a.

    b.

    c.

SKILLS AND TOOLS

1. Upper Classica's neighbor to the north, Northern Classica, (called No. Classica for short) is in long-run economic equilibrium. Data from the economy's aggregate production function is provided in the table.

Real Output ($ Trillions)	Employment (Millions)
0	0
9	20
16	40
21	60
24	80
25	100

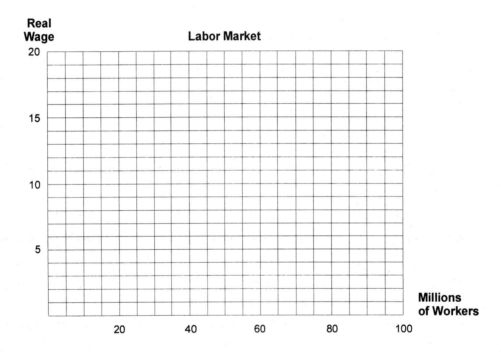

a. Plot the aggregate production function for No. Classica on the following page.

b. Labor demand in No. Classica is given by the equation

$$L^D_1 = 90 - 5W$$

where W is the real wage and L^D_1 is the number of workers (in millions) demanded.

Plot the labor demand curve above.

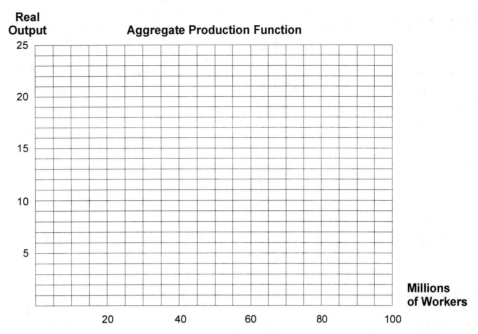

c. Labor supply in No. Classica is given by the equation

$$L^S_1 = 10W - 60.$$

Plot the labor supply curve in the appropriate panel.

d. Given the information in parts (a) through (c), the equilibrium real wage in No. Classica is _____ dollars. The equilibrium level of employment is _____ million workers, and potential output is _____ trillion dollars. Labor productivity is _____.

e. Large segments of No. Classica's labor force have been under-educated and under-skilled for years. To improve the situation, the government instituted a crash program of guaranteed student loans. It reasoned that better-educated workers would be more productive and so more attractive employees to the country's businesses. If the government is right and the policy succeeds, it will shift the labor demand curve to the (right/left). Suppose that the policy *is* successful and that businesses now want to hire exactly 30 million more workers than they did before at every level of the real wage. Plot the new labor demand curve in No. Classica.

f. After successful implementation of the policy in (e), the equilibrium real wage in No. Classica is _____ dollars. The equilibrium level of employment is _____ million workers, and full-employment real output is _____ trillion dollars. Labor productivity is _____. Compared to the economy's original equilibrium described in part (d), this policy targeting labor demand has (increased/decreased) the real wage, (increased/decreased) employment, and (increased/decreased) real output in No. Classica. Labor productivity has (increased/decreased).

g. Suppose the government now decides that too few people are in the labor force. To change that, the government decides to institute a broad range of policies to increase the reward for working, and to increase the hardship of not working. If successful, such policies as these will shift the labor supply curve to the (right/left). Suppose that the policies are *so* successful that now, at every real wage, there are 60 million more workers willing to work than there were before. Plot the new labor supply curve in No. Classica.

h. After successful implementation of the policy in (g), the equilibrium real wage in No. Classica is _____ dollars. The equilibrium level of employment is _____ million workers, and real output is _____ trillion dollars. Labor productivity is _____. Compared to the economy's previous equilibrium described in part (f), this policy targeting labor supply has (increased/decreased) the real wage, (increased/decreased) employment, and (increased/decreased) real output in No. Classica. Labor productivity has (increased/decreased).

i. To assess the combined effects of the policies directed at labor demand and labor supply, we may compare the economy's final equilibrium described in part (f), to its original equilibrium described in part (d). Making that comparison, we see that as a result of both policies combined, the real wage in No. Classica has (increased/decreased) from _____ to _____, while employment has (increased/decreased) from _____ to _____. At the same time, real output has (increased/decreased) from _____ to _____, and labor productivity has (increased/decreased) from _____ to _____. Ordinarily, this (increase/decrease) in labor productivity will be associated with a(n) (increase/decrease) in the average standard of living in No. Classica.

2. The economy of Duplicata has many similarities with No. Classica. The economy's labor demand curve, labor supply curve, and aggregate production function are all graphed on the following pages. In the graphs, the real wage is in dollars per hour, employment is in millions of workers, and real output is in trillions of dollars.

a. When Duplicata is in long run economic equilibrium, what is:

The equilibrium real wage? _____

The equilibrium level of employment? _____

Potential output? _____

Labor productivity? _____

The government recently announced a range of plans to stimulate investment and so increase the economy's capital stock. The Ministry of Economics has predicted that, if successful, the economy's aggregate production function would no longer be described by the graph in the lower panel. Instead, they predict that the new aggregate production function will be described by data in the following table.

Real Output ($ Trillions)	Employment (Millions)
0	0
13	20
20	40
24	60
25	80

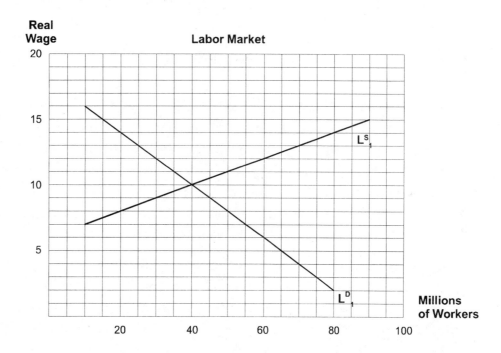

b. Plot the new aggregate production function for Duplicata on the following page.

c. If labor demand and labor supply remain as depicted, while the aggregate production function shifts as predicted in part (b), the equilibrium real wage will (rise/be unaffected/fall), employment will (rise/be unaffected/fall), real output will (rise/be unaffected/fall), and labor productivity will (rise/be unaffected/fall). Specifically, the equilibrium real wage will be _____, employment will be _____, and real output will be _____. Labor productivity will be _____.

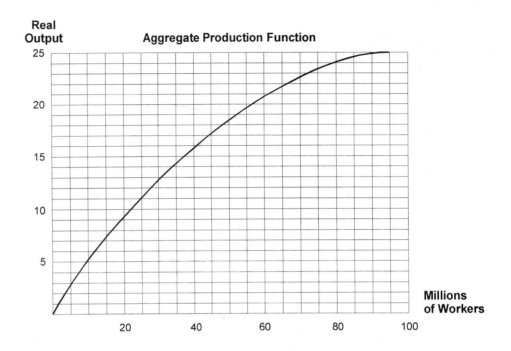

d. The new government promised to expand employment, as well as investment, but it is concerned that labor productivity might decline. If the government pursues policies that increase labor supply, employment will (increase/remain unchanged/decrease) and the real wage will (increase/remain unchanged/decrease). If it pursues policies that increase labor demand, employment will (increase/remain unchanged/decrease) and the real wage will (increase/remain unchanged/decrease). Either way, along the new aggregate production function, labor productivity will (increase/remain unchanged/decrease)..

e. The government has thought this all out and determined that as long as labor productivity falls no lower than the level it was when the government took office—the level you described in part (a)—it can get either policy in part (d) adopted. From part (a), we note that labor productivity was originally at _____. To keep labor productivity at *exactly* that level, the government could increase labor demand until it intersected the labor supply curve L^S_1 at a wage of _____ and employment level of _____. Alternatively, it could increase labor supply until it intersected labor demand curve L^D_1 at a wage of _____ and employment level of _____. Either way, labor productivity would remain at a level of _____.

15-MINUTE PRACTICE TEST

Set a timer, giving yourself just 15 minutes to answer all of the following questions. To see what you *really* know and remember, take the test at least a day *after* you've read the chapter in the text and completed the exercises in this study guide.

Multiple Choice: Circle the letter in front of the single best answer.

1. A nation's standard of living is best measured by its
    a. real GDP.
    b. real GDP per capita.
    c. output per worker.
    d. capital per worker.
    e. investment per capita.

2. Which of the following policies promotes growth by directly shifting the labor supply curve rightward?
    a. A decrease in the budget deficit
    b. A decrease in the corporate profits tax rate
    c. A cut in income tax rates
    d. A cut in the capital gains tax rate
    e. Tax incentives for firm spending on R & D

3. As employment rises along a given aggregate production function,
    a. output falls.
    b. productivity falls.
    c. labor force participation falls.
    d. all of the above.
    e. none of the above.

4. Which of the following directly causes the aggregate production function to shift upward?
    a. An increase in human capital
    b. An increase in physical capital
    c. Technological change
    d. All of the above
    e. None of the above

5. Productivity increases when
    a. investment increases.
    b. the capital stock increases.
    c. the capital stock increases faster than the population.
    d. the capital stock increases faster than employment.
    e. the labor force increases faster than the population.

6. Which of the following would tend to increase the pace of technological change?

    a. A decrease in the life span of patents
    b. Decreasing the capital gains tax rate
    c. Increasing the budget deficit
    d. Imposing a special tax on household saving
    e. Imposing a special tax on R & D

7. Which of the following policies would shift the demand for funds curve rightward in the loanable funds market, and at the same time promote more rapid economic growth?

    a. An increase in the budget deficit
    b. A decrease in the budget deficit
    c. An investment tax credit
    d. Imposing a special tax on income from wages
    e. None of the above

8. The "budgetary costs" of economic growth refers to the

    a. part of the government's budget devoted to growth-enhancing projects.
    b. part of business firms' budgets devoted to growth enhancing projects.
    c. part of households' budgets devoted to increasing their income in the future.
    d. fact that many growth-enhancing policies require decreases in tax rates and tax revenue
    e. myth that only government, and not the private sector, contributes to economic growth.

9. The "consumption cost" of economic growth refers to the

    a. increased pollution caused by rising living standards.
    b. increased use of oil and other scarce natural resources as living standards rise.
    c. need to cut back on government spending in order to promote economic growth.
    d. need to shift resources into the consumption-goods sector in order to promote growth.
    e. sacrifice of consumption goods needed to increase production of capital goods to promote growth.

10. Which of the following enables a less developed country to make use of a combination of consumption and capital goods beyond its PPF?

    a. Foreign assistance
    b. Shifting resources away from producing consumption goods and toward producing capital goods
    c. Decreasing the growth rate of the population
    d. Technological change
    e. A rightward shift of the labor supply curve

True/False: For each of the following statements, circle T if the statement is true or F if the statement is false.

T (F) 1. Economic growth is an example of a "free lunch": higher growth gives society benefits, with no associated cost.

(T) F 2. When output grows more slowly than the population, real GDP per capita—which we call the average standard of living—will fall.

T (F) 3. Increases in employment, with a constant capital stock, tend to raise productivity.

T (F) 4. An investment tax credit promotes economic growth primarily by inducing firms to hire more workers, thus moving the economy along its aggregate production function.

(T) F 5. A decrease in the budget deficit promotes economic growth primarily by lowering interest rates, which increases investment and speeds growth in the capital stock.

T (F) 6. Technological change is one of those things that just "happens," and there is virtually nothing the government can do to speed it up.

(T) F 7. One way to speed growth in real GDP is to pass more laws and create more regulations to promote worker safety, a clean environment, and other social goals.

T (F) 8. Less developed countries with very low growth rates typically suffer from a poor infrastructure and very low population growth rates.

CHAPTER 9

ECONOMIC FLUCTUATIONS

Fill in each blank with the appropriate word or phrase from the list provided in the word bank. (For a challenge, fill in as many blanks as you can *without* using the word bank.)

_____boom_____   1. A period during which real GDP exceeds full-employment GDP.

_____disequilibrium_____   2. A situation in which a market does not clear—quantity supplied is not equal to quantity demanded.

_____spending shock_____   3. A change in spending that ultimately affects the entire economy.

Word Bank

boom
disequilibrium

spending shock

CHAPTER HIGHLIGHTS

Fill in the blanks with the appropriate words or phrases. If you have difficulty, review the chapter and then try again.

1. Because sudden, large shifts in the _____labor_____ curve and in the _____demand_____ curve are unlikely to occur, and because they could not accurately describe the facts of booms and recessions, the classical model cannot explain fluctuations through shifts in the _____labor_____ and _____demand_____ curves.

2. We cannot explain the facts of _____short_____-run economic fluctuations with a model in which the labor market always _____clears_____. This is why the classical model, which assumes that the labor market always _____clears_____, does a poor job of explaining the economy in the _____short_____ run.

3. At every point along the labor supply curve, the wage rate tells us the _____opportunity cost_____ of working for the last worker to enter the labor force.

4. At every point along the labor demand curve, the ___wage rate___ tells us the benefit obtained by some firm from the last worker hired.

5. At the ___equilibrium___ level of employment, all opportunities for mutually beneficial trade in the labor market have been exploited.

6. During a recession, the labor market is in disequilibrium, and the benefit from hiring another worker is ___greater___ than the opportunity cost to that worker.

7. In recessions, there are incentives to ___rise___ the level of employment, because the benefit to firms from additional employment is ___greater___ than the opportunity cost to workers. These incentives help explain why recessions do not last forever.

8. In booms, there are incentives to ___decrease___ the level of employment, because the benefit to firms from some who have been hired is ___lower___ than the opportunity cost to those workers. These incentives help explain why booms do not last forever.

9. When a positive shock causes a boom, firms operate—temporarily—at ___higher than___-normal rates of utilization. As a consequence, employment rises above its normal, full-employment level.

10. Over time, firms that have experienced an increase in demand will return to ___normal___ utilization rates, and employment will fall back to its normal, full-employment level.

11. When an adverse shock causes a recession, firms operate—temporarily—at ___lower than___-normal rates of utilization. As a consequence, employment drops below its normal, full-employment level.

12. Over time, firms that have experienced a decrease in demand will return to ___normal___ utilization rates, and employment will rise back to its normal, full-employment level.

IMPORTANT CONCEPTS

Write a brief answer below each of the following items.

1. A leftward shift of the labor supply curve would cause a decrease in employment and output. In spite of this, we cannot attribute real world recessions to such shifts. List two reasons why not.

    a.

    b.

2. In a recession, which is greater: the opportunity cost of working for the next worker to be hired, or the benefit to some firm from hiring one more worker? Which is greater in a boom?

    Recession : benefit to firm

    Boom : opp. cost to worker

3. Briefly, how do your answers to the previous question help explain why booms and recessions do not last forever?

SKILLS AND TOOLS

For each item, follow the instructions, write the correct answer in the blank, or circle the correct answer.

1. Upandown is an economy often buffeted by shocks. Right now, however, things are pretty quiet. Labor demand and labor supply in Upandown are given by the equations

$$L^S = 10W$$

$$L^D = 240 - 10W$$

where W is the hourly real wage in dollars and L^D and L^S are millions of workers demanded and supplied, respectively.

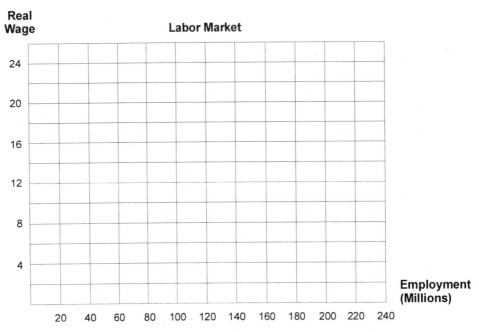

a. Plot the labor demand and labor supply curves in Upandown. In the long run, we should
    expect to see a prevailing equilibrium wage of _____ per hour and
    equilibrium employment of _____ million workers.

Recently, one of those financial doomsday books, *Day of Reckoning*, has soared to
number one on the best-seller lists. The author's dire predictions of economic disaster have
been the talk of worried executives in board rooms around the country, and many have
already cut back on their production and hiring plans. As a result, total employment in
Upandown has declined to 80 million workers.

b. When employment is 80 million, the labor market is in (equilibrium/ disequilibrium).
    The typical firm in Upandown is operating at a rate of utilization that is (above/just equal
    to/below) what is normal for that firm. The economy of Upandown is (in a boom/in long
    run equilibrium/in a recession).

c. Some of the people have begun to worry that things will never get back to normal. But
    those who study the labor market carefully have made some important observations.
    They note that with 80 million workers employed, the opportunity cost of working for
    that 80-millionth worker is _____ dollars per hour. At the same time, the
    benefit obtained by some firm from hiring that worker is _____ dollars per
    hour. Because under current condition the benefit to some firms from hiring additional
    workers (exceeds/equals/is exceeded by) the opportunity cost of working for those
    workers, mutually beneficial changes in employment (are/are not) possible. Over time,
    we would therefore expect to see firms (increase/keep steady/decrease) the number of
    workers they hire. As a result, employment in Upandown should (rise above/remain
    stable at/fall below) 80 million workers.

d. As these changes occur, the benefit firms derive from hiring additional workers will (increase/remain unchanged/decrease) while the opportunity cost of working for additional workers will (increase/remain unchanged/decrease). In the long run, we should expect to see total employment in Upandown at the level of _____ million workers, and the wage at the level of _____ dollars per hour. Under these conditions, the benefit to some firm of hiring an additional worker will be _____ dollars per hour, while the opportunity cost of working for the last worker employed will be _____ dollars per hour. Under these conditions, additional employment (would/would not) result in mutual gain for firms and workers. The labor market would again be in (equilibrium/disequilibrium) and the economy of Upandown would once again be in (a recession/long run equilibrium/a boom).

2. Labor demand and labor supply in Upandown are still given by the equations at the beginning of the previous problem. In what follows, refer to the graph you plotted there.

   a. From that graph, we know that in the long run, we should expect to see a prevailing equilibrium wage of _____ per hour and equilibrium employment of _____ million workers.

   Just when things seemed finally back to normal in Upandown, the government announced an immediate major increase in military spending to counter growing threats from the country's disgruntled neighbor, Downenout. Very quickly, employment grew to 160 million workers.

   b. When employment is at 160 million, the labor market is in (equilibrium/ disequilibrium). The typical firm in Upandown is operating at a rate of utilization that is (above/just equal to/below) what is normal for that firm. The economy of Upandown is (in a boom/in long run equilibrium/in a recession).

   c. People had never seen employment so high, and many thought it would stay that high forever. Once again, however, those who study the labor market carefully were able to make some important observations. First, they noted that in order to have attracted 160 million workers into the workforce, the real wage firms pay had to have (risen/fallen) from _____ dollars to _____ dollars per hour. With the wage at that level, the opportunity cost of working for that last 160-millionth worker would be _____ dollars per hour, while the benefit obtained by some firm from that worker is _____ dollars per hour. Because under current conditions the benefit to some firm from the last worker hired (exceeds/equals/is exceeded by) the wage the firm must pay to attract that worker, firms have an incentive to (hire more workers/keep employment steady/let some workers go). Over time, we would therefore expect to see firms (increase/keep steady/decrease) the number of workers they employ. As a result, employment in Upandown should (rise above/remain stable at/fall below) 160 million workers.

d. In the long run, we should expect to see total employment in Upandown at the level of
_____ million workers, and the wage at the level of _____
dollars per hour. Under these conditions, the benefit to some firm of hiring an additional
worker will be _____ dollars, while the opportunity cost of working for the
last worker employed will be _____ dollars. Under these conditions, the
labor market would again be in (equilibrium/disequilibrium) and the economy of
Upandown would once again be in (a recession/long run equilibrium/a boom).

10-MINUTE PRACTICE TEST

Set a timer, giving yourself just ten minutes to answer all of the following questions. To see what
you *really* know and remember, take the test at least a day *after* you've read the chapter in the
text and completed the exercises in this study guide.

Multiple Choice: Circle the letter in front of the single best answer.

1. A boom is a period during which output
    a. is rising.
    b. is recovering from a recession.
    c. exceeds full-employment output.
    d. is falling.
    e. hits bottom during a recession.

2. Real world recessions can be explained by
    a. shifts in labor demand.
    b. shifts in labor supply.
    c. changes in the labor market equilibrium.
    d. all of the above.
    e. none of the above.

3. At each level of employment, the labor supply curve tells us the
    a. opportunity cost of working for the last worker hired.
    b. benefit to some firm from the last worker hired.
    c. difference between the last worker's opportunity cost of working and the benefit he/she
        provides to some firm.
    d. equilibrium level of employment in the labor market.
    e. level of employment that a firm would hire during "normal" utilization.

4. The classical model cannot explain booms and recessions because it assumes that
    a. spending shocks can push the economy away from equilibrium.
    b. markets always clear.
    c. the labor supply curve slopes upward and the labor supply curve slopes downward.
    d. there is only one type of labor in the economy.
    e. neither the labor supply curve nor the labor demand curve can shift.

5. In a recession, the last worker hired
   a. has an opportunity cost of working greater than the benefit he/she provides for some firm.
   b. has an opportunity cost of working less than the benefit he/she provides for some firm.
   c. has an opportunity cost of working equal to the benefit he/she provides for some firm.
   d. has an opportunity cost of working greater than the wage that he/she is paid.
   e. provides a benefit to some firm that is smaller than the wage that he/she is paid.

6. In the real world, booms seem to be caused by
   a. sudden rightward shifts in the labor supply curve.
   b. sudden rightward shifts in the labor demand curve.
   c. spending shocks.
   d. all of the above.
   e. none of the above.

True/False: For each of the following statements, circle T if the statement is true or F if the statement is false.

T   F   1. During recessions, employment is unusually low and the unemployment rate is unusually high.

T   F   2. A leftward shift in the labor demand curve would occur if fewer people wanted to work at any given wage.

T   F   3. The classical model makes assumptions about the economy that make sense in the short run, but not the long run.

T   F   4. In a boom, the opportunity cost of working for the last worker hired is greater than the benefit that worker provides to some firm.

T   F   5. During a recession, firms typically operate at below-normal rates of labor utilization.

CHAPTER 10

THE SHORT-RUN MACRO MODEL

Fill in each blank with the appropriate word or phrase from the list provided in the word bank. (For a challenge, fill in as many blanks as you can *without* using the word bank.)

_____ 1. A macroeconomic model that explains how changes in spending can affect real GDP in the short run.

_____ 2. The part of household income that remains after paying taxes.

_____ 3. A positively-sloped relationship between real consumption spending and real disposable income.

_____ 4. The part of consumption spending that is independent of income; also, the vertical intercept of the consumption function.

_____ 5. The amount by which consumption spending rises when disposable income rises by one dollar.

_____ 6. Shows aggregate consumption spending at each level of income or GDP.

_____ 7. The sum of spending by households, business firms, the government and foreigners on final goods and services produced in the U.S.

_____ 8. In the short-run macro model, the level of output at which output and spending are equal.

_____ 9. The amount by which equilibrium real GDP changes as a result of a one-dollar change in autonomous consumption, investment, government purchases or net exports.

_____ 10. Forces that reduce the size of the expenditure multiplier and diminish the impact of spending shocks.

Word Bank

aggregate expenditure (AE)
automatic stabilizers
autonomous consumption spending
consumption function
consumption-income line

disposable income
equilibrium GDP
expenditure multiplier
marginal propensity to consume (MPC)
short-run macro model

CHAPTER HIGHLIGHTS

Fill in the blanks with the appropriate words or phrases. If you have difficulty, review the chapter and then try again.

1. In the short run, the relationship between _____ and _____ goes both ways: _____ depends on _____ , and _____ depends on _____ .

2. The marginal propensity to consume (MPC) is (1) the slope of the _____ function; (2) the change in consumption divided by the change in _____ income; or (3) the amount by which consumption spending rises when _____ income rises by one dollar.

3. The MPC is always greater than _____ and less than _____ .

4. When the government collects a fixed amount of taxes from households, the line representing the relationship between consumption and income shifts downward by the amount of the tax times the _____. The slope of this line, however, is unaffected by taxes, and is equal to the _____.

5. When a change in _____ causes consumption spending to change, we move along the consumption-income line. When a change in _____ causes consumption spending to change, the line will shift.

6. In the short-run macro model, we define investment spending as _____ and equipment purchases by business firms, and _____ construction. _____ investment is treated as unintentional and undesired, and is therefore excluded from our definition of investment spending.

7. In the simple, short-run macro model of this chapter, _____ spending, _____ purchases, and _____ are all regarded as given values, determined by forces _____ of the model.

8. Aggregate expentirue is the sum of spending by households, _____ , the government, and the _____ sector on _____ goods and services produced in the United States. Or, in symbols, AE = _____ .

9. When income increases, aggregate expenditure will rise by the _____ times the change in income.

10. When aggregate expenditure is less than GDP, output will _____ in the future. Thus, any level of output at which aggregate expenditure is less than GDP cannot be the _____ GDP.

11. When aggregate expenditure is greater than GDP, output will _____ in the future. Thus, any level of output at which aggregate expenditure exceeds GDP cannot be the _____ GDP.

12. In the short-run, equilibrium GDP is the level of output at which _____ and _____ are equal.

13. The change in inventories during any period will always equal _____ minus _____.

14. A _____ line is a translator line: It allows us to measure any horizontal distance as a vertical distance instead.

15. At any output level at which the aggregate expenditure line lies below the _____ line, aggregate expenditure is less than GDP. If firms produce any of these output levels, their _____ will grow, and they will _____ output in the future.

16. At any output level at which the aggregate expenditure line lies above the _____ line, aggregate expenditure exceeds GDP. If firms produce any of these output levels, their _____ will decline, and they will _____ their output in the future.

17. _____ GDP is the output level at which the aggregate expenditure line intersects the _____ line. If firms produce this output level, their inventories will not change, and they will be content to continue producing the same level of output in the future.

18. In the short-run macro model, cyclical unemployment is caused by insufficient _____. As long as _____ remains low, production will remain low, and unemployment will remain high.

19. In the short-run macro model, the economy can overheat because _____ is too high. As long as _____ remains high, production will exceed potential output, and unemployment will be unusually low.

20. The expenditure multiplier is the number by which a change in spending (e.g., investment spending) must be multiplied to get the change in _____.

21. For any value of the MPC, the formula for the expenditure multiplier is

    _____.

22. Just as increases in spending cause equilibrium GDP to _____ by a multiple of the change in spending, decreases in spending cause equilibrium GDP to _____ by a multiple of the change in spending.

23. Changes in investment, government purchases, net exports or autonomous consumption lead to a _____ effect on GDP. The expenditure _____ is what we multiply the initial change in spending by in order to get the change in equilibrium GDP.

24. An increase in _____ consumption spending, investment spending, government purchases or _____ will shift the _____ line upward by the increase in spending, causing equilibrium GDP to rise. The increase in GDP will equal the initial increase in spending times the _____ multiplier.

25. An automatic _____ reduces the size of the expenditure multiplier and therefore _____ the impact of spending shocks on the economy. As a result, the economy is _____ stable.

26. In the long run, the expenditure multiplier has a value of _____: No matter what the change in spending or taxes, output will return to _____, so the change in equilibrium GDP will be _____.

27. In the long run, an increase in the desire to save leads to faster economic growth and rising living standards. In the short run, however, it can cause a (an) _____ that pushes output _____ its potential.

IMPORTANT CONCEPTS

Write a brief answer below each of the following items.

1. List the four components of aggregate expenditure used in this chapter's short-run macro model.

   a.

   b.

   c.

   d.

2. Give the mathematical formulas for each of the following:

   a. The relationship between consumption (C) and disposable income (DI):

   b. The formula for the expenditure multiplier:

   c. The special formula for the tax multiplier (if you've read Appendix 2 of this chapter):

3. List five different changes that could cause equilibrium GDP to *decrease*.

   a.

   b.

   c.

   d.

   e.

4. If the MPC were equal to zero, and government spending increased by $100 billion, would equilibrium GDP increase? If yes, by how much. If no, why not?

SKILLS AND TOOLS

1. Data on income (GDP), disposable income, and consumption spending are presented below. All figures are in billions of dollars.

Income or GDP ($ Billions)	Tax Collections ($ Billions)	Disposable Income ($ Billions)	Consumption Spending ($ Billions)
_____	_____	2,000	2,500
_____	_____	2,500	2,750
4,000	_____	_____	3,000
_____	_____	3,500	3,250
5,000	_____	4,000	3,500
5,500	_____	_____	3,750
_____	_____	5,000	4,000
_____	_____	5,500	4,250
7,000	_____	_____	4,500
7,500	_____	_____	4,750

a. Suppose taxes are $1,000 at every level of real income. Complete the table.

b. On the grid provided, plot the consumption-income line corresponding to these data.

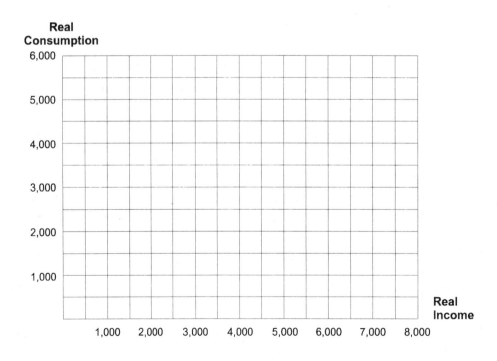

c. What is the marginal propensity to consume (MPC) in this economy? _____

d. If taxes increase from $1,000 to $2,000 at every level of real income, then real disposable income will (increase/decrease) by _____ dollars at every level of real income. Because the MPC in this economy is equal to _____, this means that consumption spending will (increase/decrease) by exactly _____ dollars at every level of real income. In the graph above, this means that an increase in taxes from $1,000 to $2,000 will cause the consumption-income line to shift (upward/downward) by exactly _____ at every level of real income.

e. Plot the new consumption-income line when taxes are $2,000. What is the marginal propensity to consume equal to now? _____

f. Following the increase in taxes just described, in order to restore the consumption-income line to its original position in part (b), there would have to be an (increase/decrease) in the interest rate, an (increase/decrease) in household wealth, or an (increase/decrease) in consumer optimism.

2. In the table below, consumption and income data have been carried forward from the previous problem.

a. If planned investment spending by businesses is fixed at $600 billion, government purchases are fixed at $400 billion, and net exports are fixed at $250 billion, complete the table.

Income or GDP ($ Billions)	Consumption Spending ($ Billions)	Investment Spending ($ Billions)	Government Purchases ($ Billions)	Net Exports ($ Billions)	Aggregate Expenditure ($ Billions)
3,000	2,500	_____	_____	_____	_____
3,500	2,750	_____	_____	_____	_____
4,000	3,000	_____	_____	_____	_____
4,500	3,250	_____	_____	_____	_____
5,000	3,500	_____	_____	_____	_____
5,500	3,750	_____	_____	_____	_____
6,000	4,000	_____	_____	_____	_____
6,500	4,250	_____	_____	_____	_____
7,000	4,500	_____	_____	_____	_____
7,500	4,750	_____	_____	_____	_____

b. At any level of GDP, aggregate expenditure, or *AE*, is equal to the sum _____.
    When aggregate expenditure exceeds GDP, output will tend to (rise/remain constant/fall).
    When aggregate expenditure is less than GDP, output will tend to (rise/remain
    constant/fall). Output will remain constant, and the economy will have achieved its short
    run equilibrium GDP, when aggregate expenditure (exceeds/equals/is exceeded by) GDP.

c. On the grid provided, plot the "45-degree line," or translator line, along which GDP and
    real aggregate expenditure are equal to each other. Then, using the data from part (a), plot
    the economy's aggregate expenditure line.

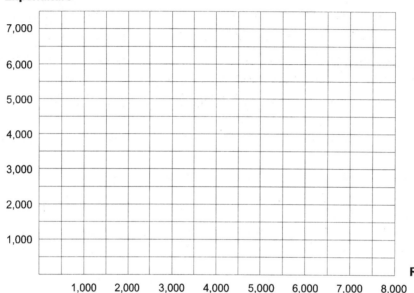

d. The equilibrium GDP in this economy (is/is not) equal to $2,500 billion. When real GDP
    is $2,500 billion, aggregate expenditure is _____ billion. Because aggregate
    expenditure is (greater than/equal to/less than) GDP, firms are producing (more output
    than/as much output as/less output than) they are selling. As a result, the change in firms'
    inventories is equal to _____ billion dollars. Over time, this means that firms
    will (increase their output/keep their output constant/decrease their output) and GDP will
    (rise/remain constant/fall).

e. The equilibrium GDP in this economy (is/is not) equal to $4,500 billion. When real GDP
    is $4,500 billion, aggregate expenditure is _____ billion. Because aggregate
    expenditure is (greater than/equal to/less than) GDP, firms are producing (more output
    than/as much output as/less output than) they are selling. As a result, the change in firms'
    inventories is equal to _____ billion dollars. Over time, this means that firms
    will (increase their output/keep their output constant/decrease their output) and GDP will
    (rise/remain constant/fall).

    f. The equilibrium GDP in this economy (is/is not) equal to $6,500 billion. When real GDP is $6,500 billion, aggregate expenditure is _____ billion. Because aggregate expenditure is (greater than/equal to/less than) GDP, firms are producing (more output than/as much output as/less output than) they are selling. As a result, the change in firms' inventories is equal to _____ billion dollars. Over time, this means that firms will (increase their output/keep their output constant/decrease their output) and GDP will (rise/remain constant/fall).

    g. Suppose that (potential) full-employment output in this economy is $5,000 billion. Then the short-run equilibrium levels of output and employment are (above/the same as/below) the long run equilibrium levels of output and employment. In this case, aggregate spending is (too high/just right/too low), and the economy will experience (over-heating/steady income/unemployment) in the short run. To achieve full-employment, the government could (increase/hold constant/decrease) government purchases in order to (increase/hold constant/decrease) aggregate expenditure and cause equilibrium GDP to (rise to/stay steady at/fall to) its full employment equilibrium level.

3. The aggregate expenditure line for some economy is plotted below. Axes measure billions of dollars.

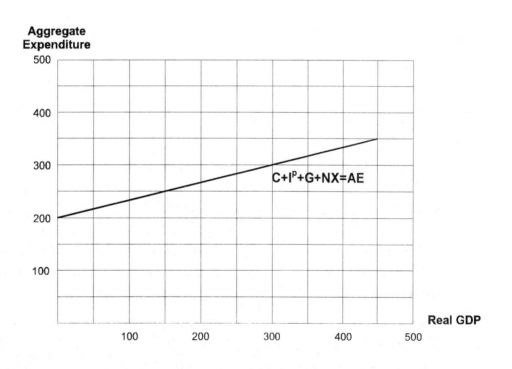

    a. What is the value of the marginal propensity to consume in this economy?

      _____

    b. What is the value of the expenditure multiplier in this economy? _____

c. What is the short run equilibrium level of real GDP? _____

d. If full employment output in this economy is $150 billion, investment would have to
    (increase/decrease) by _____ dollars to bring equilibrium output to this level.
    Alternatively, government purchases would have to (increase/decrease) by
    _____ to achieve the same result.

e. If either of the spending changes in part (d) occurred, the economy's aggregate
    expenditure line would (shift downward/shift upward) by exactly _____
    billion dollars at every level of real GDP. On the graph on the previous page, plot the
    aggregate expenditure line that would result.

4. You have been trying to collect information on the MPC and the short run expenditure
    multiplier in six different countries. You've been able to come up with only a few of the items
    you want, and you've arranged them in the table below. Note that the last three columns
    report the change in equilibrium GDP that results from changes in different kinds of
    expenditure.

			Change in Equilibrium GDP due to:			
Country	**MPC**	**Multiplier**	$\Delta I^p = +200$	$\Delta G = -100$	$\Delta a = +400$	$\Delta NX = -150$
1	0.40	_____	_____	_____	_____	-250
2	_____	2.00	_____	-200	800	_____
3	0.60	_____	500	-250	_____	_____
4	_____	_____	800	_____	1,600	-600
5	_____	_____	_____	-500	2,000	_____
6	_____	_____	2,000	_____	4,000	_____

a. Complete the table.

b. Suppose we know that in Country 4, short run equilibrium output is $1,000 billion and
    potential output is $1,400 billion. Then in order to increase output to its full employment
    level, the government could (increase/decrease) government purchases by
    _____ billion dollars. Because the expenditure multiplier in Country 4 is
    _____, this change in spending will cause equilibrium real output to rise by
    _____ billion dollars.

c. Suppose we know that in Country 5, short run equilibrium output is $1,000 billion and
    potential output is $800 billion. Then in order to decrease output to its full employment
    level, the government could (increase/decrease) government purchases by
    _____ billion dollars. Because the expenditure multiplier in Country 1 is
    _____, this change in spending will cause equilibrium real output to fall by
    _____ billion dollars.

(This question refers to material found in Appendix 1 to the chapter.)

5. Consumption spending (C), investment spending (I^P), government purchases (G), and taxes (T) are given by the following equations:

$$C = 85 + (1/2) Y_D$$
$$I^P = 55$$
$$G = 75$$
$$T = 30.$$

All figures are in billions of dollars.

a. In the consumption function given above, the term Y_D stands for _____. If Y stands for total income or GDP, Y_D is calculated by (adding/subtracting) the amount of ($C/I^P/G/T/Y$) from ($C/I^P/G/T/Y$).

b. What is the equation for the consumption-income line? _____

c. What is the equation for aggregate expenditure, AE? _____

d. What is the value of equilibrium GDP? _____

e. What is the MPC in this economy? _____

f. What is the value of the expenditure multiplier? _____

g. Suppose that investment spending rises to $70 billion. What will be the resulting equilibrium GDP? _____

(This question refers to material found in Appendix 2 to the chapter.)

6. The equation for aggregate expenditures in an economy is

$$AE = 5{,}000 + 0.5Y$$

Where AE is aggregate expenditure ($C+I^P+G+NX$) and Y is GDP, both in billions of dollars.

a. What is the MPC in this economy ? ___.5___

b. What is the expenditure multiplier in this economy? ___$\frac{1}{1-.5} = \frac{1}{.5} = 2$___

c. What is the tax multiplier in this economy? _____

d. What is equilibrium GDP in this economy? _____

e. Potential output in this economy is $12,000 billion. To bring equilibrium GDP to this full-employment level, the government could (increase/decrease) taxes by _____ billion dollars. Alternatively, the government could (increase/decrease) government purchases by _____ billion dollars, instead.

15-MINUTE PRACTICE TEST

Set a timer, giving yourself just 15 minutes to answer all of the following questions. To see what you *really* know and remember, take the test at least a day *after* you've read the chapter in the text and completed the exercises in this study guide.

Multiple Choice: Circle the letter in front of the single, best answer.

1. Disposable income is equal to
    a. income plus taxes.
    b. income minus taxes.
    c. income plus saving minus taxes.
    d. consumption plus government purchases minus taxes.
    e. consumption plus saving minus taxes.

2. If the MPC in an economy equals 0.8, and disposable income falls by $100, consumption spending will fall by
    a. $0.80.
    b. $8.00.
    c. $20.00.
    d. $80.00.
    e. $500.00.

3. Which of the following will cause the consumption-income line to shift upward?
    a. An increase in income
    b. An increase in taxes
    c. An increase in government spending
    d. All of the above
    e. None of the above

4. The increase in inventories during the year is equal to
    a. $C + I + G + NX$.
    b. $AE - I$.
    c. $AE - (C + I + G + NX)$.
    d. $GDP - AE$.
    e. $C + I + G + NX - GDP$.

5. In the short-run macro model, if the MPC equals 0.9 and investment spending rises by $200 billion, then equilibrium GDP will rise by
    a. $20 billion.
    b. $180 billion.
    c. $90 billion.
    d. $1,000 billion.
    e. $2,000 billion.

6. In the short-run macro model, a rise in autonomous consumption (*a*) causes
   a. a movement rightward along the consumption-income line.
   b. equilibrium real GDP to increase by an amount equal to the rise in autonomous consumption.
   c. equilibrium real GDP to increase by a multiple of the rise in autonomous consumption.
   d. equilibrium real GDP to decrease by an amount equal to the rise in autonomous consumption.
   e. no change in equilibrium real GDP.

7. Automatic stabilizers are
   a. well-timed government policy changes that help keep the economy stable at full employment.
   b. forces in the economy that increase the size of the expenditure multiplier.
   c. spending shocks that move in the opposite direction of, and help to neutralize, other spending shocks.
   d. actions taken by foreign governments that help stabilize our own economy.
   e. none of the above.

8. In the short-run macro model, an increase in saving has the effect of
   a. speeding economic growth.
   b. increasing consumption.
   c. increasing investment.
   d. increasing government spending.
   e. causing a recession.

9. In the short-run macro model, cyclical unemployment is caused by insufficient
   a. labor supply.
   b. labor demand.
   c. spending.
   d. saving.
   e. taxes.

10. If the MPC were equal to zero, the expenditure multiplier would be
    a. less than zero.
    b. zero.
    c. between zero and one.
    d. one.
    e. greater than one.

True/False: For each of the following statements, circle T if the statement is true or F if the statement is false.

T   F   1. Autonomous consumption spending is represented graphically as the vertical intercept of the consumption function.

T   F   2. An increase in disposable income causes the consumption function to shift upward.

T   F   3. An increase in taxes causes the consumption-income line to shift downward.

T   F   4. In the short-run macro model, an increase in autonomous consumption spending, investment spending, net exports, government purchases, or taxes will all cause equilibrium GDP to increase.

T   F   5. When aggregate expenditure is less than GDP, the change in inventories is negative and GDP will increase in future periods.

T   F   6. In the short-run macro model, an increase in government spending will cause an increase in employment.

T   F   7. All else being equal, the larger the MPC, the larger will be the multiplier.

T   F   8. As the economy adjusts to its new equilibrium after an increase in government spending, consumption spending rises.

CHAPTER 11

THE BANKING SYSTEM AND THE MONEY SUPPLY

Fill in each blank with the appropriate word or phrase from the list provided in the word bank.
(For a challenge, fill in as many blanks as you can *without* using the word bank.)

liquidity   1. The property of being easily converted into cash.

cash   2. Currency and coins held outside of banks.

Demand Deposits   3. Checking accounts that do not pay interest.

_M1_   4. A standard measure of the money supply, including cash in the hands of the public, checking account deposits, and travelers' checks.

_M2_   5. A measure of the money supply including cash in the hands of the public, checking accounts, travelers' checks, savings account balances, noninstitutional money market mutual fund balances, and small time deposits.

financial int.   6. A business firm that specializes in brokering between savers and borrowers.

Balance Sheet   7. A financial statement showing assets, liabilities, and net worth at a point in time.

BOND   8. An IOU issued by a corporation or government agency when it borrows funds.

LOAN   9. An IOU issued by a household or unincorporated business when it borrows funds.

Reserves   10. Vault cash plus balances held at the Fed.

_RR_   11. The minimum amount of reserves a bank must hold, depending upon the amount of its deposit liabilities.

RRR   12. The minimum fraction of checking account balances that banks must hold as reserves.

net worth   13. The difference between assets and liabilities.

central bank   14. A nation's principal monetary authority.

FOMC   15. A group of Federal Reserve officials that establishes U.S. monetary policy.

Discount Rate   16. The interest rate the Fed charges on loans to banks.

Open Market Op   17. Purchases or sales of bonds by the Federal Reserve System.

ER   18. Reserves held beyond those required.

DD Mult.   19. The number by which a change in reserves is multiplied to determine the resulting change in demand deposits.

Run on Bank   20. An attempt by many of a bank's depositors to withdraw their funds.

Panic   ~~Run on Bank~~   21. A situation in which depositors attempt to withdraw funds from many banks simultaneously.

Word Bank

balance sheet

banking panic

bond

cash in the hands of the public

central bank

demand deposit multiplier

demand deposits

discount rate

excess reserves

Federal Open Market Committee

financial intermediary

liquidity

loan

M1

M2

net worth

open market operations

required reserve ratio

required reserves

reserves

run on the bank

CHAPTER HIGHLIGHTS

Fill in the blanks with the appropriate words or phrases. If you have difficulty, review the chapter and then try again.

1. An asset is considered liquid if it can be converted to _____ quickly and at little cost. An illiquid asset, by contrast, can be converted to _____ only after a delay, or at considerable cost.

2. The money supply measure M1 consists of _____ in the hands of the public plus _____ deposits plus other _____ deposits plus _____ checks. In the text, it is assumed that the money supply consists of just two components: _____ in the hands of the public and _____ deposits.

3. One column of a bank's balance sheet lists the banks assets—anything of value that the bank _____. The other column lists the bank's liabilities—amounts that the bank _____.

4. The more funds a bank's customers hold in their checking accounts, the more the bank must hold as _____.

5. When the Fed wishes to increase or decrease the money supply, it buys or sells _____ bonds. These actions are called _____.

6. The demand deposit multiplier is the number by which we must multiply the injection of _____ to get the total change in demand deposits.

7. For any value of the required reserve ratio (RRR), the formula for the demand deposit multiplier is _____.

8. After an injection of reserves, the demand deposit multiplier stops working—and the money supply stops incr4easing—only when all the reserves injecfted are being held by banks as _____ reserves.

9. While other tools can affect the money supply, open market operations have two advantages over them: precision and _____. This is why open market operations remain the Fed's primary means of changing the money supply.

10. Most economists believe that if we want the freedom from banking panics provided by the _____, we must also accept the strict regulation and close monitoring of banks provided by the Fed and other agencies.

IMPORTANT CONCEPTS

Write a brief answer below each of the following items.

1. List the four components of the M1 measure of the money supply.

   a.

   b.

   c.

   d.

2. State whether each of the following would be listed on a bank's balance sheet, by writing *yes* or *no*. If *yes*, state whether the entry would occur on the assets side or the liabilities side of the balance sheet.

   a. _____ The real estate and buildings in the bank's possession.

   b. _____ Government bonds held by the bank.

   c. _____ Mortgage loans the bank has made to private citizens.

   d. _____ The income earned by the bank during the year.

   e. _____ Checking accounts held by the bank's customers.

   f. _____ Cash in the bank's vault.

   g. _____ The bank's net worth.

3. The membership of the Fed's Board of Governors and its Federal Open Market Committee (FOMC) are not identical. What is the difference?

4. State briefly how each of the following helps determine the composition of the Federal Open Market Committee.

   a. The President of the United States

   b. The U.S. Senate

   c. The 5,000 member banks

SKILLS AND TOOLS

1. The following are data on the economy of Minnewaska:

Cash in the hands of the public	=	$402
Public's credit limit on all credit cards	=	$136
Demand deposits and all other checkable deposits	=	$693
Money market mutual funds	=	$618
Travelers' checks	=	$8
Large time deposits	=	$512
Small time deposits	=	$971
Public's stock market holdings	=	$1,069
Savings-type accounts	=	$256

   a. What is the value of M1 for this economy? _____

   b. What is the value of M2 for this economy? _____

   c. What entries in the table are not counted as part of the economy's money stock?

   _____

2. Minnewaska has a central bank which, by coincidence, also happens to be called "the Fed." One of its leading commercial banks, First Bank of Minnewaska, holds the demand deposits of 15,000 individuals. Each individual has placed $10,000 in the bank. The government has borrowed $55 million from the bank. The bank has $45 million in loans to private citizens and $20 million in loans to various companies on its books. First Bank of Minnewaska owns the property and building where it is located, and these have a total assessed value of $21 million. The bank holds $12 million in vault cash and has $18 million in its account at the Fed. First Bank of Minnewaska *always* stays loaned up (i.e. never holds excess reserves).

   a. Complete the balance sheet for First Bank of Minnewaska.

First Bank of Minnewaska

Assets		Liabilities and Net Worth	
_____		_____	
_____		_____	
_____			
_____			
_____			
_____			
Total Assets	_____	Total Liabilities plus Net Worth	_____

   b. What is First Bank's net worth? _____

   c. How much in reserves does First Bank hold? _____ Since this bank always remains loaned up, we can assume that all reserves it holds are (excess/required) reserves. Thus, we can deduce that in Minnewaska the required reserve ratio is _____.

3. Minnewaska's Fed has decided to buy a $5,000 government bond from SabreTooth Trading, a bond dealer. SabreTooth has received a check for $5,000 from the Fed and deposited it into its checking account at First Bank of Minnewaska.

   a. As a result of the Fed's action, reserves at First Bank of Minnewaska have (increased/decreased) by _____ dollars. If the required reserve ratio is 0.2, this means that First Bank of Minnewaska has (excess reserves/deficient reserves) in the amount of _____ dollars. Now, the bank (can make new loans/must call in loans) in the amount of _____ dollars. This transaction alone causes the money supply of Minnewaska to (increase/decrease) by _____ dollars.

b. Fill in the blanks to describe the impact of the transaction in part (a) upon First Bank of Minnewaska's balance sheet. Model your answer on similar tables in the text, using + to indicate an increase, and − to indicate a decrease.

Changes in First Bank of Minnewaska's Balance Sheet

Action	Changes in Assets	Changes in Liabilities
Fed buys $5,000 bond from Sabre-Tooth Trading, which deposits $5,000 check from Fed deposits into its checking account:	_5000_ in reserves	_5000_ in demand deposits
First Bank (lends out excess reserves/calls in loans) in amount of _____ dollars:	− _4000_ in reserves + _4000_ in loans	
The total effect on First Bank from beginning to end:	_1000_ in reserves _4000_ in loans	_5000_ in demand deposits

c. Suppose First Bank of Minnewaska lends its excess reserves to Cindy, who then deposits the proceeds into her checking account at *Bank Too!* of Minnewaska. As a result of this action, reserves at *Bank Too!* have (increased/decreased) by _____ dollars. If the required reserve ratio is 0.2, *Bank Too!* now has (excess reserves/deficient reserves) of _____ dollars. Now, the bank (can make new loans/must call in loans) of _____ dollars. This transaction, alone, causes the money supply of Minnewaska to (increase/decrease) by _____ dollars.

d. Fill in the blanks to describe the impact of the transaction in part (c) upon the following balance sheet for *Bank Too!*, using + to indicate an increase, and − to indicate a decrease.

Changes in *Bank Too!*'s Balance Sheet

Action	Changes in Assets	Changes in Liabilities
Cindy deposits _____ loan check into her checking account:	_____ in reserves	_____ in demand deposits
Bank Too! (lends out excess reserves/calls in loans) in amount of _____ dollars:	_____ in reserves _____ in loans	
The total effect on *Bank Too!* from beginning to end:	_____ in reserves _____ in loans	_____ in demand deposits

e. Assume that banks in Minnewaska always keep themselves fully loaned up (that is, they never hold excess reserves). Suppose, also, that anyone receiving a loan deposits the proceeds in one of Minnewaska's banks, and anyone paying off a loan withdraws the amount due from one of Minnewaska's banks. Still supposing that the required reserve ratio is 0.2, complete the following table to trace the impact of the Fed's action throughout the banking system. (Note that the last column indicates *cumulative* change, as in the text.)

Round	Change in Demand Deposits at This Bank	Change in Demand Deposits at All Banks
First Bank of Minnewaska	_____	_____
Bank Too!	_____	_____
Bank 3	_____	_____
Bank 4	_____	_____
Bank 5	_____	_____
Bank 6	_____	_____
Bank 7	_____	_____
Bank 8	_____	_____
…		
All Other Banks	_____	_____

f. As each bank in turn (makes new loans/calls in old loans) it (creates/extinguishes) demand deposits. In the end, the cumulative effect of all banks' actions, together, is a multiple (increase/decrease) in Minnewaska's money supply equal to _____ times the original change in reserves

4. Always in the bond market, Minnewaska's Fed has just sold a $2,000 bond to SabreTooth Trading. To buy the bond, SabreTooth has withdrawn $2,000 from its checking account at First Bank of Minnewaska.

a. As a result of the Fed's actions reserves at First Bank of Minnewaska have (increased/decreased) by _____ dollars. If the required reserve ratio is 0.2, this means that First Bank of Minnewaska has (excess reserves/deficient reserves) in the amount of _____ dollars. Now, the bank (can make new loans/must call in loans) in the amount of _____ dollars. This transaction alone causes the money supply to (increase/decrease) by _____ dollars.

b. Fill in the blanks to describe the impact of the transaction in part (a) upon First Bank of Minnewaska's balance sheet. Model your answer on similar tables in the text, using + to indicate an increase, and – to indicate a decrease.

Changes in First Bank of Minnewaska's Balance Sheet

Action	Changes in Assets	Changes in Liabilities
Fed sells $2,000 bond to SabreTooth, which pays with $2,000 check drawn on its checking account at First Bank.	–2000 in reserves	–2000 in demand deposits
First Bank (lends out excess reserves/~~calls in loans~~) in amount of 1600 dollars:	+ 1600 in reserves – 1600 in loans	
The total effect on First Bank from beginning to end:	– 400 in reserves – 1600 in loans	2000 in demand deposits

c. Assume that banks in Minnewaska always keep themselves fully loaned up. Suppose, also, that anyone receiving a loan deposits the proceeds in one of Minnewaska's banks, and anyone paying off a loan withdraws the amount due from one of Minnewaska's banks. Still supposing that the required reserve ratio is 0.2, complete the following table to trace the impact of the Fed's action throughout the banking system. (Note that the last column indicates *cumulative* change, as in the text.)

Round	Change in Demand Deposits at This Bank	Change in Demand Deposits at All Banks
First Bank of Minnewaska	_____	_____
Bank 2	_____	_____
Bank 3	_____	_____
Bank 4	_____	_____
Bank 5	_____	_____
Bank 6	_____	_____
Bank 7	_____	_____
Bank 8	_____	_____
…		
All Other Banks	_____	_____

d. As each bank in turn (makes new loans/calls in old loans) it (creates/extinguishes) demand deposits. In the end, the cumulative effect of all banks' actions, together, is a multiple (increase/decrease) in Minnewaska's money supply equal to _____ times the original change in reserves

5. Information on banking systems in six different countries has been arranged in the table below. The last three columns report the eventual change in the country's money supply resulting from open market sales or purchases by the country's central bank in the amounts indicated. Assume that all commercial banks remain always fully loaned up, and that cash in the hands of the public does not change.

Country	RRR	Demand Deposit Multiplier	Change in Money Supply due to Open Market:		
			Sale of $200	Purchase of $100	Sale of $400
1	0.1	_____	_____	_____	–4,000
2	0.2	_____	_____	_____	_____
3	_____	2.5	_____	_____	_____
4	_____	_____	–400	_____	–800
5	0.8	_____	_____	125	_____
6	_____	1.0	–200	_____	_____

a. Complete the table.

b. If the central bank in Country 2 wants to increase the money supply by $1000, it must (increase/decrease) reserves by the amount of _____ dollars. One way to do this is through open market (sales/purchases). Alternatively, the central bank could achieve the same increase in the money supply by an appropriate (increase/decrease) in the required reserve ratio, or an appropriate (increase/decrease) in the discount rate. However, if the central bank chooses to use open market operations to increase the money supply by $1000, it will be required to (buy/sell) securities from the public in the amount of _____ dollars.

c. If the central bank in Country 4 wants to decrease the money supply by $1,000, it must (increase/decrease) reserves by the amount of _____ dollars. One way to do this is through open market (sales/purchases). Alternatively, the central bank could achieve the same decrease in the money supply by an appropriate (increase/decrease) in the required reserve ratio, or an appropriate (increase/decrease) in the discount rate. However, if the central bank chooses to use open market operations to decrease the money supply by $1,000, it will be required to (buy/sell) securities from the public in the amount of _____ dollars.

15-MINUTE PRACTICE TEST

Set a timer, giving yourself just 15 minutes to answer all of the following questions. To see what you *really* know and remember, take the test at least a day *after* you've read the chapter in the text and completed the exercises in this study guide.

Multiple Choice: Circle the letter in front of the single, best answer.

1. Which of the following assets is the most liquid?
   a. Checking account funds
   b. Government bonds
   c. Money market funds
   d. Real estate
   e. Rare stamps

2. Which of the following assets are included in the M1 measure of the money supply?
   a. Checking account funds
   b. Cash in a bank's vault
   c. Reserves that banks hold at the Fed
   d. All of the above
   e. None of the above

3. Which of the following items would *not* be listed on a bank's balance sheet?
   a. The bank's net worth
   b. Property and buildings that the bank owns
   c. Loans the bank has made to others
   d. Government bonds in the bank's possession
   e. The bank's income during the year

4. If the required reserve ratio is 0.10, and a bank has $10 million in customer demand deposits, then its required reserves are

   a. $100,000.
   b. $90,000.
   c. $1 million.
   d. $9 million.
   e. $10 million.

5. Which of the following is a member of the Federal Open Market Committee?

   a. The President of the New York Federal Reserve Bank
   b. The U.S. Secretary of the Treasury
   c. The President of the United States
   d. The Majority Leader of the U.S. Senate
   e. All of the above

6. Which of the following would tend to *increase* the U.S. money supply?

   a. An increase in the discount rate
   b. A decrease in the required reserve ratio
   c. A sale of government bonds by the FOMC
   d. All of the above
   e. None of the above

7. When a bank makes a loan, the bank's balance sheet will immediately show

   a. an increase in both assets and liabilities.
   b. a decrease in both assets and liabilities.
   c. an increase in assets and a decrease in liabilities.
   d. an increase and a decrease in assets.
   e. an increase and a decrease in liabilities.

8. Under the simple assumptions of the chapter (that the public does not change its holdings of cash, and that banks do not hold excess reserves), if the required reserve ratio is 0.2, and the Fed purchases $10 million in government bonds, then the money supply will

   a. decrease by $2 million.
   b. decrease by $5 million.
   c. increase by $2 million.
   d. increase by $5 million.
   e. increase by $50 million.

9. One important reason that banking panics have been eliminated in the United States since the Great Depression is that

   a. banks are more free today than in the 1930s to lend as they see fit.
   b. all commercial banks are now strictly regulated by individual states, rather than loosely regulated by the Federal government.
   c. the FDIC insures customer deposits.
   d. the government stands ready to suspend all banking activity at a moment's notice.
   e. all of the above.

10. The most common method used by the Fed to change the money supply is
    a. changes in the discount rate.
    b. alterations of FDIC regulations.
    c. changes in the required reserve ratio.
    d. open market operations.
    e. sales and purchases of gold.

True/False: For each of the following statements, circle T if the statement is true or F if the statement is false.

T F 1. The M2 measure of the money supply contains all of the assets in M1, plus some additional assets.

T F 2. A bank's balance sheet lists, among other items, the bank's income and expenses during the year.

T F 3. The U.S. President selects all of the members of the Federal Open Market Committee.

T F 4. An important function of the Fed is to supervise and regulate commercial banks.

T F 5. When the Fed sells government bonds, the money supply decreases.

  T F 6. If banks increase their holdings of excess reserves as the money supply expands, the demand deposit multiplier will be larger than 1/RRR.

T F 7. Most economists argue that FDIC protection alone cannot eliminate banking panics; we must also eliminate banking regulation.

T F 8. The number of bank failures in the United States has steadily increased through the twentieth century.

CHAPTER 12

THE MONEY MARKET AND THE INTEREST RATE

Fill in each blank with the appropriate word or phrase from the list provided in the word bank. (For a challenge, fill in as many blanks as you can *without* using the word bank.)

wealth constraint 1. At any point in time, wealth is fixed.

MD curve 2. A curve indicating how much money will be willingly held at each interest rate.

MS curve 3. A line showing the total quantity of money in the economy at each interest rate.

excess S M 4. The amount of money households and firms are holding minus the amount demanded at a particular interest rate.

_E D B_ 5. The amount of bonds households and firms want to hold minus the amount they are actually holding at a particular interest rate.

Fed Fund R 6. The interest rate charged for loans of reserves among banks.

Word Bank

excess demand for bonds	money demand curve
excess supply of money	money supply curve
federal funds rate	wealth constraint

Fill in the blanks with the appropriate words or phrases. If you have difficulty, review the chapter and then try again.

1. An individual's quantity of money demanded is the amount of _wealth_ that the individual chooses to hold as money, rather than as other assets.

2. When you hold money, you bear an opportunity cost—the ___interest___ you could have earned.

3. In the chapter, we assume that individuals choose how to divide their wealth between two assets: (1) money, which can be used as a ___means of pay___ but earns no ___interest___; and (2) bonds, which earn ___interest___, but cannot be used as a ___m o p___.

4. The (economy-wide) demand for money is the amount of total ___wealth___ in the economy that all households and businesses, together, choose to hold as ___cash___ rather than as bonds.

5. A change in the ___r___ moves us along the money demand curve. A change in money demand caused by something other than a change in ___r___ (such as real income or the price level) will cause the curve to shift.

6. Open market purchases of bonds inject reserves into the banking system, and shift the money ___supply___ curve to the ___up right___ by a multiple of the reserve injection. Open market sales have the opposite effect: They withdraw reserves from the system and shift the money ___supply___ curve to the ___left___ by a multiple of the reserve withdrawal.

7. ___eq___ in the money market occurs when the quantity of money people are actually holding (quantity supplied) is equal to the quantity of money they want to hold (quantity demanded).

8. When there is an excess supply of money in the economy, there is also an excess ___demand___ for bonds.

9. When the price of bonds rises, the interest rate ___① ↓___; when the price of bonds falls; the interest rate ___① ↑___.

10. If the Fed increases the money supply by ___buying___ government bonds, the interest rate ___↓___. If the Fed decreases the money supply by ___sell___ government bonds, the interest rate ___↑___. By controlling the money supply through purchases and sales of bonds, the Fed can also control the interest rate.

11. When the Fed increases the money supply, the interest rate _____↓_____, and spending on three categories of goods increases: plant and equipment, new housing, and consumer _consumer/dur_ (especially automobiles). When the Fed decreases the money supply, the interest rate _____↑_____, and these categories of spending fall.

12. An increase in government purchases, which by itself shifts the aggregate expenditure line _____↑_____ , also sets in motion forces that shift it _____↓_____ .

13. In the short run, an increase in government purchases causes real GDP to rise, but not by as much as it would have risen if the _____↑_____ had not increased.

14. When effects in the money market are included in the short-run macro model, an increase in government purchases causes the interest rate to _____↑_____ and crowds out some private _investment_ spending. It may also crowd out consumption spending.

15. Increases in government purchases, investment, net exports and autonomous consumption, as well as decreases in taxes, all shift the aggregate expenditure line upward. Real GDP rises, but so does the _____↑_____, so the rise in equilibrium GDP is smaller than would occur if the _____↑_____ remained constant.

16. Decreases in government purchases, investment, and autonomous consumption, as well as increases in taxes, all shift the aggregate expenditure line downward. Real GDP falls, but so does the _____↑_____, so the decline in equilibrium GDP is smaller than would occur if the _____↑_____ remained constant.

17. Our view of the interest rate depends on the time period we are considering. In the long run, we view the interest rate as determined in the market for _loanable fund$_ , where household saving is lent to businesses and the government. In the short run, we view the interest rate as determined in the _money_ market, where wealth holders adjust their wealth between money and bonds, and the Fed participates by controlling the money supply.

18. A general expectation that interest rates will rise (i.e., that bond prices will _____↓_____) in the future will cause the money demand curve to shift _____→_____ in the present. This will cause the interest rate to _____↑_____ in the present.

IMPORTANT CONCEPTS

Write a brief answer below each of the following items.

1. In the chapter, households must allocate their wealth between two types of assets. What are they?

   a. *Money*

   b. *Bonds*

2. Each of the following events shifts either the money demand or the money supply curve. For each event, write (1) which curve shifts and (2) whether it shifts rightward or leftward.

   a. Income decreases

   D.   shift lef

   b. The Fed sells government bonds to bond dealers

   S   shift   left

   c. The Fed lowers the required reserve ratio

   MS shift right

   d. People *expect* the interest rate to rise in the near future

   D shift Right

   e. People *expect* the Fed to increase the money supply in the near future

   D shift right

   f. The government reduces taxes

   MS → right

3. Suppose that neither consumption spending nor investment spending were influenced by changes in the interest rate. How would this affect the Fed's ability to change GDP by using monetary policy?

4. Suppose the Fed *decreases* the money supply. State whether each of the following will increase, decrease, or remain unchanged.

   a. GDP _____

   b. The interest rate _____

   c. The price of bonds _____

   d. Investment spending _____

   e. Consumption spending _____

   f. The quantity of money demanded _____

SKILLS AND TOOLS

For each of the following items, follow the instructions, write the correct answer in the blank, or circle the correct answer.

1. Suppose the demand for money is given by

$$M^d = 750 - 50r$$

   where M^d is the quantity of money demanded (in billions of dollars) and r is the interest rate in percentage points.

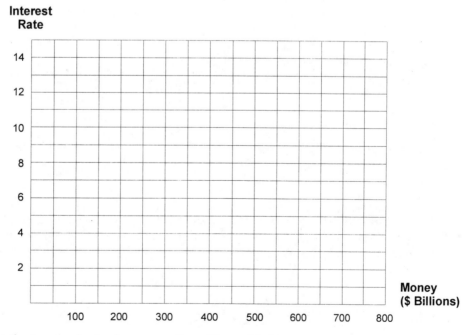

   a. Plot the money demand curve on the grid provided.

b. Plot the money supply curve if the Fed sets the money supply at $400 billion.

c. At an interest rate of 12%, the quantity of money demanded is (greater than/less than) the quantity of money supplied. There is (excess demand/excess supply) in the money market equal to dollars. This implies that when the interest rate is 12%, there is (excess demand/excess supply) in the bond market equal to _____ billion dollars. In response, as people try to (buy more/sell more) bonds, the price of bonds will (rise/fall). As it does, the interest rate in the money market will (rise/fall).

d. At an interest rate of 4%, the quantity of money demanded is (greater than/less than) the quantity of money supplied. There is (excess demand/excess supply) in the money market equal to _____ dollars. This implies that when the interest rate is 4%, there is (excess demand/excess supply) in the bond market equal to _____ dollars. As people try to (buy more/sell more) bonds, the price of bonds will (rise/fall). As it does, the interest rate in the money market will (rise/fall).

e. The equilibrium interest rate is _____ percent. At this rate of interest, the quantity of money people want to hold is (less than/equal to/greater than) the amount of money in circulation. At the same time, the bond market is in (equilibrium/disequilibrium). We can infer that the quantity of bonds people want to hold at the prevailing price of bonds is (greater than/equal to/less than) the quantity of bonds available.

2. The demand for money is

$$M^d = 650 - 50r$$

where M^d is the quantity of money demanded (in billions of dollars) and r is the interest rate in percentage points. The money supply has been set at

$$M^S_1 = \$250 \text{ billion.}$$

Suppose that all demand deposits are held in commercial banks, and that all commercial banks are subject to fractional reserve requirements where the required reserve ratio is

$$RRR = 0.5.$$

a. On the grid on the following page, plot the money demand and money supply curves. What is the equilibrium interest rate? _____

b. The Fed has decided it wants the interest rate to be 4%. To achieve that interest rate, the Fed must (increase/decrease) the money supply by _____ billion, from its current level of $M^S_1 = \$250$ billion to a new level of _____ billion dollars. If the Fed decides to use open market operations to change the money supply, it will have to (buy/sell) bonds. With $RRR = 0.5$ the demand deposit multiplier is _____. Thus, to achieve an interest rate of 4% the Fed will have to (buy/sell) bonds in the amount _____ billion.

c. Illustrate your answer to (b) by plotting the new money supply curve. Label your curve M^S_2.

d. Wait a minute. They changed their minds: the Fed would really rather the interest rate were 10%. To achieve that interest rate, the Fed must (increase/decrease) the money supply by _____ billion, from its current level of $M^S_1 = \$250$ billion to a new level of _____ billion. If the Fed decides to use open market operations to change the money supply, it will have to (buy/sell) bonds. With $RRR = 0.5$ the demand deposit multiplier is _____. Thus, to achieve an interest rate of 10% the Fed will have to (buy/sell) bonds in the amount of _____ billion.

e. Illustrate your answer to (d) by plotting the new money supply curve. Label your curve M^S_3.

3. In **Panel A**, the money market is in equilibrium at an interest rate of 6%. In **Panel B**, aggregate expenditure at an interest rate of 6% intersects the "45-degree" translator line where real GDP is $4,500 billion.

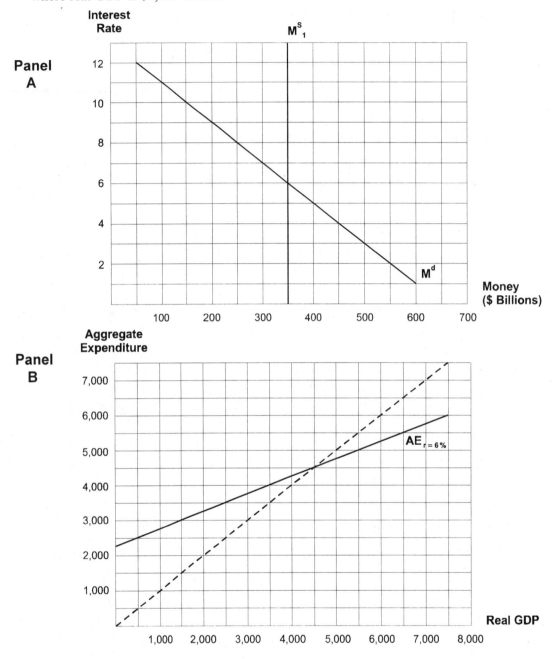

a. Suppose the Fed decides to reduce the money supply to $200 billion. As the money supply curve shifts (leftward/rightward), the equilibrium interest rate will (rise/fall) to _____ percent. This (increase/decrease) in the equilibrium interest rate will tend to (increase/decrease) interest-sensitive spending such as (consumption/ consumption and planned investment/government purchases and planned investment). These spending changes will shift the aggregate expenditure line (upward/downward) in the Panel B. Equilibrium GDP will therefore (increase/decrease) by (the same amount as/a multiple of/a fraction of) that change in spending. This change in equilibrium GDP will, itself, cause further changes in the money market. Specifically, we would expect that this change in GDP will (increase/decrease) money (supply/demand), causing the equilibrium interest rate to (rise/fall).

b. Suppose that as a result of all the actions described in part (a), the new equilibrium interest rate is 7%. On the grid, illustrate this new equilibrium in the money market.

c. Suppose that as a result of all the actions described in part (a), and given the interest rate of 7% as in part (d), the new equilibrium GDP is $2,500. Illustrate this new equilibrium by drawing in an appropriate new aggregate expenditure line parallel to the line $AE_{r=6\%}$. Label the new line $AE_{r=7\%}$.

d. The Fed's monetary policy eventually caused short-run equilibrium GDP to fall from $4,500 billion to $2,500 billion. With a careful look at the diagrams, we can see that the Fed's action caused interest sensitive spending to (rise/fall) by _____ billion from its original level.

4. In **Panel C**, the money market is in equilibrium at an interest rate of 8%. In **Panel D**, aggregate expenditure at an interest rate of 8% intersects the "45-degree" translator line where real GDP is $150 billion.

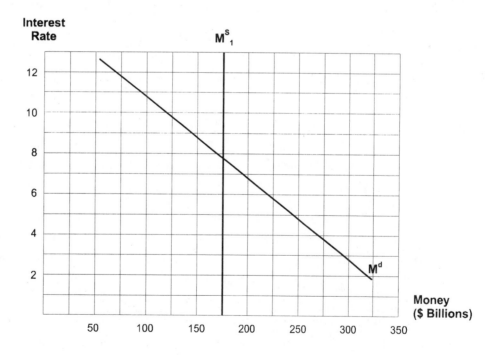

**Panel
D**

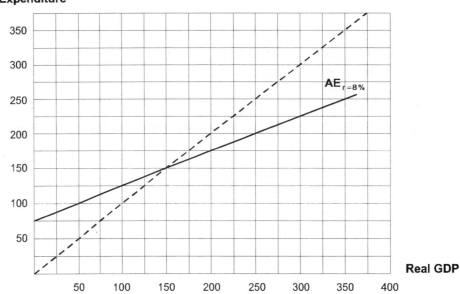

a. Suppose government purchases are increased by $75 billion. Assuming for the moment
    that this action has no impact whatsoever on the money market, the aggregate
    expenditure line in the Panel D would shift (upward/downward) by exactly
    _____ billion at every level of real GDP. Equilibrium GDP would then rise
    from _____ billion to _____ billion. Draw in a dashed line to
    illustrate an *AE* curve consistent with the situation just described.

b. We know, however, that any change in GDP as described in part (a) will normally have
    an affect on the money market. In general, increases in GDP will (increase/decrease)
    money (demand/supply), shifting the money (demand/supply) curve
    (leftward/rightward). As a result, the interest rate will (rise/fall) in the money market.
    This change in the interest rate, all other thing equal, will cause a(n) (increase/decrease)
    in interest-sensitive spending. This would be reflected by a(n) (upward/downward) shift
    in the dashed *AE* line drawn in part (a).

c. Suppose that after all effects have been accounted for, the new short-run equilibrium
    level of GDP is $250 billion and the interest rate is 10 percent. Illustrate this in the Panel
    C with the appropriate shift in the money demand or money supply curve, and in the
    Panel D with an appropriate *AE* curve parallel to the one you drew for part (a).

d. From a careful look at the diagrams, we can see that the original $75 billion increase in
    government purchases caused the interest rate to (rise/fall) which, in turn, (crowded
    out/stimulated additional) private investment and consumption spending in the amount of
    _____ billion. Had there been no affect on the money market, the $75 billion
    increase in government purchases would have increased equilibrium GDP from

_____ billion to _____ billion. However, when we take account of the impact on the market and the equilibrium interest rate, equilibrium GDP rose, instead, from _____ billion to _____ billion. Thus, when we take account of the impact increased spending and income will have on the money market, we can see that fiscal policy (will still cause GDP to rise but by a smaller multiple of any given change in spending/cannot cause GDP to change at all).

15-MINUTE PRACTICE TEST

Set a timer, giving yourself just 15 minutes to answer all of the following questions. To see what you _really_ know and remember, take the test at least a day _after_ you've read the chapter in the text and completed the exercises in this study guide.

Multiple Choice: Circle the letter in front of the single best answer.

1. The opportunity cost of money is
   a. the time and trouble it takes to obtain money, such as the time it takes to go to an ATM machine and make a withdrawal.
   b. the risk that money can be lost or stolen.
   c. the interest that could have been earned if one's wealth were held in bonds, instead of money.
   d. the inconvenience of switching out of bonds and into money, and vice versa.
   e. all of the above.

2. The money demand curve slopes downward because a rise in the interest rate causes
   a. the Fed to decrease the quantity of money in circulation.
   b. bonds to become more attractive.
   c. the opportunity cost of holding money to decrease.
   d. investment spending to decrease.
   e. consumption spending to decrease.

3. The money supply curve
   a. slopes downward, because the Fed increases the money supply whenever the interest rate falls.
   b. slopes downward, because the Fed decreases the money supply whenever the interest rate falls.
   c. slopes upward, because a rise in the interest rate makes people want to hold more of their wealth in the form of money.
   d. slopes upward, because a rise in the interest rate makes people want to hold less of their wealth in the form of money.
   e. is vertical, because the Fed sets the money supply at whatever level it wants to.

4. If there is an excess demand for money, then
   a. there is also an excess supply of bonds.
   b. the interest rate is lower than its equilibrium value.
   c. the interest rate will rise.
   d. all of the above.
   e. none of the above.

5. Monetary policy works as follows: when the Fed purchases government bonds,
   a. the money supply decreases, the interest rate rises, and investment spending falls.
   b. the money supply increases, the interest rate rises, and investment spending falls.
   c. the money supply decreases, the interest rate falls, and investment spending rises.
   d. the money supply increases, the interest rate falls, and investment spending rises.
   e. the money supply decreases, the interest rate falls, and investment spending falls.

6. When we include the money market with the short-run macro model, an increase in government purchases causes
   a. GDP to increase.
   b. the interest rate to increase.
   c. the demand for money to increase.
   d. all of the above.
   e. none of the above.

7. When we add the money market to the short-run macro model,
   a. fiscal policy becomes completely ineffective in changing GDP.
   b. fiscal policy becomes less effective in changing GDP.
   c. monetary policy becomes completely ineffective in changing GDP.
   d. fiscal policy becomes even more effective in changing GDP.
   e. fiscal policy can change GDP, but not the interest rate.

8. If the Fed keeps the money supply unchanged, an increase in government purchases will cause
   a. the interest rate to rise.
   b. GDP to increase.
   c. investment spending to fall.
   d. all of the above.
   e. none of the above.

9. If people suddenly expect the interest rate to fall in the future, then currently,
   a. the money demand curve will shift leftward.
   b. the money supply curve will shift leftward.
   c. the price of bonds will fall.
   d. all of the above.
   e. none of the above.

10. If the Fed announces that it is about to dramatically decrease the money supply, then currently,
    a. the interest rate will fall.
    b. the money demand curve will shift leftward.
    c. the money supply curve will shift rightward.
    d. all of the above.
    e. none of the above.

True/False: For each of the following statements, circle T if the statement is true or F if the statement is false.

T   F   1. The money demand curve is vertical because the Fed determines how much money is circulating in the economy.

T   F   2. A rise in the interest rate causes the money demand curve to shift leftward.

T   F   3. When there is an excess supply of money in the economy, there is also an excess supply of bonds.

T   F   4. When bond prices rise, the interest rate falls.

T   F   5. If the Fed keeps the money supply unchanged, a decrease in government purchases causes the interst rate to drop.

T   F   6. Equilibrium in the money market occurs when the total quantity of money people are actually holding is equal to the total quantity of money that people want to hold.

T   F   7. If the Fed sells government bonds, the interest rate will fall.

T   F   8. When we include the effects of the money market, an increase in government purchases causes real GDP to rise by even more than when we ignore the money market.

CHAPTER 13

AGGREGATE DEMAND AND AGGREGATE SUPPLY

SPEAKING ECONOMICS

Fill in each blank with the appropriate word or phrase from the list provided in the word bank. (For a challenge, fill in as many blanks as you can *without* using the word bank.)

___AD___ 1. A curve indicating equilibrium GDP at each price level.

___AS___ 2. A curve indicating the price level consistent with firms' unit costs and markups for any level of output over the short run.

___SR MAC Eq.___ 3. A combination of price level and GDP consistent with both the AD and AS curves.

___D shock___ 4. Any event that causes the AD curve to shift.

___S shock___ 5. Any event that causes the AS curve to shift.

___Self correct___ 6. The adjustment process through which price and wage changes return the economy to full-employment output in the long run.

___LR AS Curve___ 7. A vertical line indicating all possible output and price-level combinations at which the economy could end up in the long run.

___Stag. flat.___ 8. The combination of falling output and rising prices.

Word Bank

aggregate demand curve (AD) curve
aggregate supply (AS) curve
demand shock
long-run aggregate supply curve

self-correcting mechanism
short-run macroeconomic equilibrium
stagflation
supply shock

CHAPTER HIGHLIGHTS

Fill in the blanks with the appropriate words or phrases. If you have difficulty, review the chapter and then try again.

1. A rise in the price level causes a(n) ___*↓*___ in equilibrium GDP. The aggregate demand (AD) curve tells us the equilibrium real GDP at any ___*P level*___.

2. When a change in ___*P level*___ causes equilibrium GDP to change, we move along the AD curve. Whenever anything other than ___*P level*___ causes equilibrium GDP to change, the AD curve itself shifts.

3. The AD curve shifts rightward when government purchases, ___*↑*___ spending, net exports or autonomous ___*consumption*___ spending increases, or when ___*tax*___ decrease.

4. The AD curve shifts leftward when government purchases, ___*↓*___ spending, net exports or autonomous ___*consumption*___ spending decreases, or when ___*tax*___ increase.

5. A(n) ___*↑*___ in the money supply shifts the AD curve rightward.
   A(n) ___*↓*___ in the money supply shifts the AD curve leftward.

6. In the chapter, it is assumed that a firm sets the price of its products as a markup over ___*cost per unit*___.

7. The average percentage ___*markup*___ in the economy is determined by competitive conditions in the economy. The competitive structure of the economy changes very slowly, so the average percentage ___*markup*___ should be somewhat stable from year to year.

8. In the short run, the price level ___*↑*___ when there is an economy-wide increase in unit costs, and the price level ___*↓*___ when there is an economy-wide decrease in unit costs.

9. For a year or so after a change in output, changes in the average nominal ___*wage*___ are less important than other forces that change unit costs.

10. In the chapter, it is assumed that changes in output have no effect on the nominal ___*wage*___ in the short run.

11. In the short run, a rise in real GDP, by causing unit costs to _____*up*_____, will also cause the price level to _____*up*_____. In the short run, a fall in real GDP, by causing unit costs to _____*down*_____, will also cause the price level to _____*down*_____.

12. The aggregate supply curve (or AS curve) tells us the _____*P level*_____ consistent with firms' unit costs and their percentage markup at any level of _____*GDP output*_____ over the short run.

13. When a change in _____*GDP*_____ causes the price level to change, we move along the AS curve. When anything other than a change in _____*GDP*_____ causes the price level to change, the AS curve itself shifts.

14. An event that causes the AD curve to shift is called a _____*Demand shock*_____. An event that causes the AS curve to shift is called a _____*Supply shock*_____.

15. When government purchases increase, the horizontal shift of the _____*Dem*_____ curve measures how much real GDP would increase if the price level remained constant. But because the price level rises, real GDP rises by _____*less*_____ than the horizontal shift in the _____*AD*_____ curve.

16. A positive demand shock—one that shifts the AD curve _____*right*_____—causes both real GDP and the price level to _____*up*_____ in the short run. A negative demand shock—one that shifts the AD curve _____*left*_____—causes both real GDP and the price level to _____*down*_____ in the short run.

17. In the short run, we treat the wage rate as given. But in the long run, the wage rate can change. When output is above full employment, the wage rate will _____*up*_____, shifting the AS curve _____*up*_____. When output is below full employment, the wage rate will _____*down*_____, shifting the AS curve _____*down*_____.

18. If a demand shock pulls the economy away from full employment, changes in the wage rate and the price level will eventually cause the economy to correct itself and return to _____*full E*_____ output.

19. Whenever a demand shock pulls the economy away from full employment, the _____*self correct*_____ mechanism will eventually bring it back. When output exceeds its full-employment level, wages will eventually _____*up*_____, causing a(n) _____*up*_____ in the price level and a(n) _____*down*_____ in real GDP until full employment is restored. When output is less than its full-employment level, wages

will eventually _____↓_____, causing a(n) _____↓_____ in the price level and a(n) _____↑_____ in real GDP until full employment is restored.

20. The self-correcting mechanism shows us that, in the _____*Long*_____ run, the economy will eventually behave as the classical model predicts.

21. In the short run, a negative supply shock shifts the AS curve _____*down left*_____, decreasing output and _____↑_____ the price level. A negative supply shock causes stagflation in the short run. A positive supply shock shifts the AS curve _____*right*_____, increasing output and _____↓_____ the price level.

22. In the long run, the economy self-corrects after a supply shock, just as it does after a demand shock. When output differs from its full-employment level, the wage rate changes, and the _____*AS*_____ curve shifts until full employment is restored.

IMPORTANT CONCEPTS

Write a brief answer below each of the following items.

1. Indicate whether each of the following increases, decreases or remains the same as we move *rightward* along an AD curve.

   a. output _____↑_____

   b. the price level _____↓_____

   c. the money supply _____*Same*_____

   d. the demand for money at any interest rate _____↓_____

   e. the interest rate _____↓_____

   f. investment spending _____↑_____

   g. government purchases _____*Same*_____

2. State whether each of the following increases, decreases or remains the same as we move *rightward* along an AS curve.

   a. output _____↑_____

   b. the price level _____↑_____

   c. the average percentage markup in the economy _____*same*_____

   d. the prices of inputs _____↑_____

e. firms' unit costs _____

f. the average nominal wage rate _____

3. For each of the following, state which curve shifts (AD or AS) and in which direction (rightward, leftward, upward or downward).

a. an increase in government purchases _____

b. an increase in taxes _____

c. an increase in the money supply _____

d. an increase in autonomous consumption spending _____

e. an increase in world oil prices _____

f. an increase in the average nominal wage _____

g. a decrease in firms' average percentage markup _____

4. In the table below, identify the *short run* impact of each event on each variable by entering *increase*, *decrease*, or *no change*.

	Event		
Short run effect on:	**the money supply decreases**	**government purchases decrease**	**world oil prices decrease**
the price level	_____	_____	_____
output	_____	_____	_____
average nominal wage	_____	_____	_____

5. In the table below, identify the *long run* impact of each event on each variable by entering *increase*, *decrease*, or *remains unchanged*. Assume that the economy begins at full-employment output. Remember to think only about *long run* effects in this table.

	Event		
Long run effect on:	**the money supply decreases**	**government purchases decrease**	**world oil prices decrease**
the price level	_____	_____	_____
output	_____	_____	_____
average nominal wage	_____	_____	_____

SKILLS AND TOOLS

For each of the following items, follow the instructions, write the correct answer in the blank, or circle the correct answer.

1. The price level in the economy is 100 and the money supply is $550 billion. Money demand depends on the interest rate and is given by the equation

$$M^d = 1050 - 50r$$

where r is the interest rate in percentage points and M^d is billions of dollars demanded.

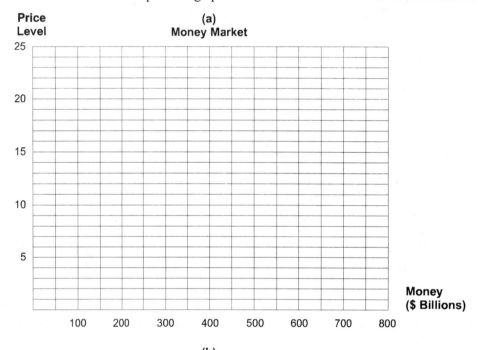

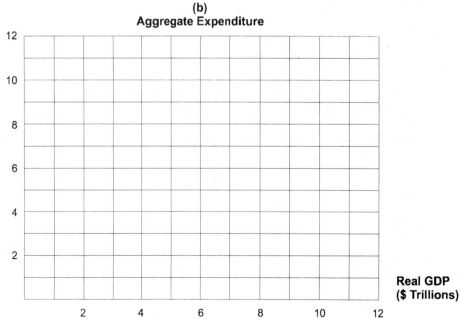

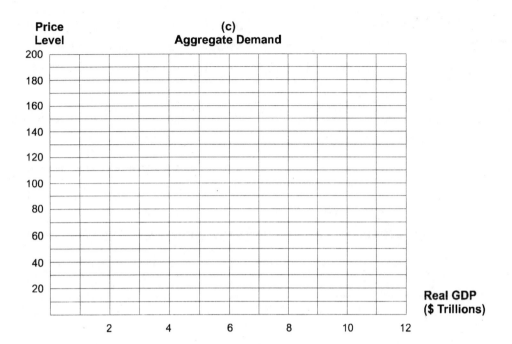

a. Plot money supply and money demand in panel (a), and label them M^S and $M^d_{P=100}$, respectively. The money market is in equilibrium when the interest rate is

_____.

b. At the interest rate from part (a), aggregate expenditure is given by the equation

$$AE = 3 + .5Y$$

where Y is the level of real GDP in trillions of dollars and AE is aggregate expenditure.

Plot aggregate expenditure in panel (b) and label it $AE_{r=10\%}$.

c. At a price level of 100, equilibrium real GDP is _____. Plot this point in panel (c) and label it A.

d. Suppose the price level increases to 130. In the money market, this will result in a (rightward/leftward) shift in the (money demand curve/money supply curve).

e. Suppose the shift described in part (d) is in the amount of $100 billion at every level of the interest rate. Plot the new money demand curve in panel (a) and label it $M^D_{P=130}$. The shift in the money demand curve will (increase/decrease) the interest rate to _____ percent.

f. The new interest rate causes interest sensitive spending to (rise/fall) and causes the aggregate expenditure line to shift (upward/downward) at every level of real GDP.

g. Suppose the shift described in part (f) is in the amount of $1 trillion at every level of real GDP. Plot the new aggregate expenditure line in panel (b) and label it $AE_{r=12\%}$. Through the multiplier process, equilibrium real GDP will (increase/decrease) to _____ trillion.

h. Looking back over questions (d) – (g), we can see that as the price level increases from 100 to 130, equilibrium real GDP (increases/decreases) from _____ trillion to _____ trillion. Plot the new point in panel (c) corresponding to a price level of 130 and label it B.

i. Suppose the price level decreases from 100 to 70. In the money market, this will result in a (rightward/leftward) shift in the (money demand curve/money supply curve).

j. Suppose the shift described in part (i) is in the amount of $100 billion at every level of the interest rate. Plot the new money demand curve in panel (a) and label it $M^D_{P=70}$. The shift in the money demand curve will (increase/decrease) the interest rate to _____ percent.

k. The new interest rate causes interest sensitive spending to (rise/fall) and causes the aggregate expenditure line to shift (upward/downward) at every level of real GDP.

l. Suppose the shift described in part (k) is in the amount of $1 trillion at every level of real GDP. Plot the new aggregate expenditure line in panel (b) and label it $AE_{r=8\%}$. Though the multiplier process, equilibrium real GDP will (increase/decrease) to _____ trillion.

m. Looking back over questions (i) – (l), we can see that as the price level decreases from 100 to 70, equilibrium real GDP (increases/decreases) from _____ trillion to _____ trillion. Plot the new point corresponding to a price level of 70 in panel (c) and label it C.

n. Connecting points A, B, and C, draw a curve in panel (c) that represents the AD curve for this economy.

2. The economy currently has an output of $7 trillion and a price level of 100.

a. Plot this point in the grid on the following page and label it A.

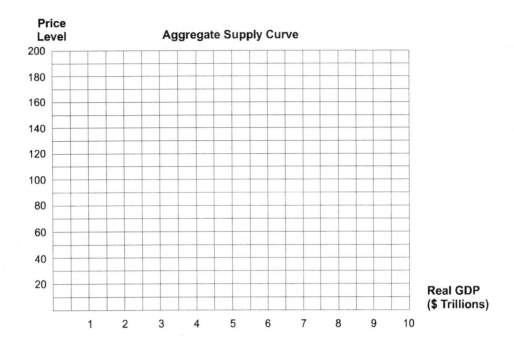

b. Suppose that the economy's real GDP increases from $7 trillion to $8.5 trillion. As a result of the increase in output, (greater/smaller) amounts of labor, capital, land, and raw materials are needed to produced each unit of output. As demand for these inputs (increases/decreases), the price of non-labor inputs will (increase/decrease). This causes unit costs to (increase/decrease). As long as the average percentage markup in the economy remains somewhat stable, the (rise/fall) in unit costs will lead firms to (raise/lower) their prices, and the price level will (increase/decrease).

c. Suppose the increase in real GDP described in part (b) changes the price level by 40. Plot the new point corresponding to a real GDP of $8.5 trillion in the space above and label it *B*.

d. Suppose that the economy's real GDP decreases from $7 trillion to $6 trillion. As a result of the decrease in output, (greater/smaller) amounts of labor, capital, land, and raw materials are needed to produced each unit of output. As demand for these inputs (increases/decreases), the price of non-labor inputs will (increase/decrease). This causes unit costs to (increase/decrease). As long as the average percentage markup in the economy remains somewhat stable, the (rise/fall) in unit costs will lead firms to (raise/lower) their prices, and the price level will (increase/decrease).

e. Suppose the decrease in real GDP described in part (d) changes the price level by 20. Plot the new point corresponding to a real GDP of $6 trillion in the space above and label it *C*.

f. Connecting points *A*, *B*, and *C*, draw a curve that represents the AS curve for this economy.

3. The full-employment output for some economy is $6 trillion. Aggregate demand and aggregate supply depend on the price level, P, according to the following equations:

$$\text{Aggregate Demand: } AD = 16 - P/10$$

$$\text{Aggregate Supply: } AS = P/10 - 4.$$

a. In the space provided, plot the AD curve, the AS curve, and full-employment output for this economy. Label them AD_1, AS_1, and Y_{FE}, respectively.

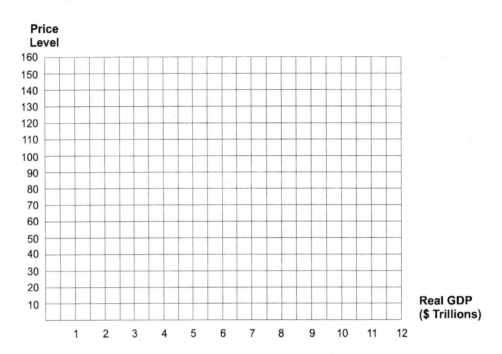

b. Is the economy in long-run equilibrium? (Yes/No). When the economy is in long-run equilibrium, the price level is _____ and real GDP is _____.

c. Suppose the Fed decreases the money supply through open market sales of bonds. This action will (increase/decrease) the interest rate, which will (increase/decrease) interest-sensitive consumption and investment spending. This results in an (increase/decrease) in real GDP and a (rightward/leftward) shift in the AD curve.

d. Suppose the shift described in part (c) is in the amount of $4 trillion at every price level. Plot the new AD curve in the space above and label it AD_2.

e. As real GDP (increases/decreases), unit costs will (increase/decrease) and the price level will (increase/decrease). As a result, money demand will (increase/decrease) and the interest rate will (rise/fall). The new interest rate will cause interest-sensitive consumption and investment spending to (increase/decrease). Thus, overall, GDP will (increase/decrease) (more/less) than the original $4 trillion shift in the AD curve.

f. In the new short-run equilibrium, real GDP is _____ trillion and the price level is _____.

g. In this short-run equilibrium, GDP is (above/below) its full-employment level. The unusually (high/low) unemployment rate drives the wage rate (up/down). As a result, the AS curve will shift (upward/downward) until a new long-run equilibrium is achieved. This will occur at a price level of _____ and real GDP of _____.

h. Plot the new AS curve described in part (g) and label it AS_2.

4. Copy onto the grid below the AD_1 curve, the AS_1 curve, and Y_{FE} from question (3).

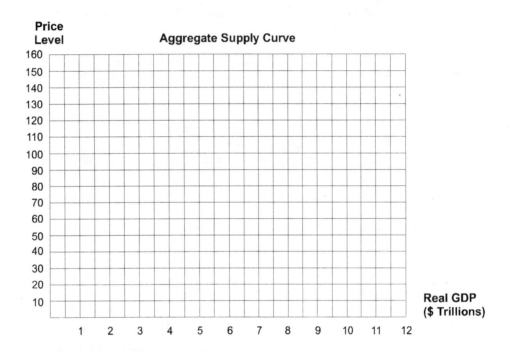

a. Suppose the economy experiences unusually good weather, resulting in bumper crop yields and falling agricultural prices. As a result, the price level will (increase/decrease) at every level of real GDP. This will shift the AS curve (upward/downward).

b. Suppose that the shift described in part (a) is in the amount of 20. Plot the new AS curve in the above grid and label it AS_2. The short-run equilibrium occurs at a price level of _____ and real GDP of _____.

c. Real GDP is now (above/below) the full-employment output for this economy. The unusually (high/low) unemployment rate drives the wage rate (up/down). As a result, the AS curve will shift (upward/downward) until a new long-run equilibrium is achieved. This occurs at a price level of _____ and real GDP of _____.

d. Plot the new AS curve described in part (c) and label it AS_3.

15-MINUTE PRACTICE TEST

Set a timer, giving yourself just 15 minutes to answer all of the following questions. To see what you *really* know and remember, take the test at least a day *after* you've read the chapter in the text and completed the exercises in this study guide.

Multiple Choice: Circle the letter in front of the single best answer.

1. At every point on the AD curve
    a. aggregate expenditure is equal to output.
    b. the demand for money is equal to the supply of money.
    c. the change in aggregate inventories is equal to zero.
    d. all of the above.
    e. none of the above.

2. A rise in the price level causes a
    a. rightward shift of the AD curve.
    b. leftward shift of the AD curve.
    c. movement rightward along the AD curve.
    d. movement leftward along the AD curve.
    e. leftward shift of the AD curve, as well as a movement leftward along the AD curve.

3. As we move rightward along the AD curve,
    a. the price level falls.
    b. the interest rate falls.
    c. investment spending increases.
    d. all of the above.
    e. none of the above.

4. According to the AS-AD model, the short-run effects of an increase in government spending include
    a. a rise in the interest rate.
    b. a fall in output.
    c. a fall in the price level.
    d. all of the above.
    e. none of the above.

5. According to the AS-AD model, the long-run effects of an increase in government spending include
    a. a drop in the interest rate.
    b. a rise in output.
    c. a rise in the price level.
    d. all of the above.
    e. none of the above.

6. The aggregate supply curve tells us
   a. the level of output at which aggregate expenditure equals output, for each possible price level.
   b. the price level consistent with firms' units costs and the average percentage markup, for each possible output level.
   c. the output level at which the demand for money is equal to the supply of money, for each possible price level.
   d. the output level at which investment spending is equal to household saving, for each possible price level.
   e. all of the above.

7. Which of the following would directly shift the AS curve upward?
   a. A decrease in the money supply
   b. An increase in the average nominal wage
   c. An increase in investment spending
   d. An increase in autonomous consumption spending
   e. An increase in output

8. Which of the following is an example of a positive demand shock?
   a. A decrease in the money supply
   b. An increase in world oil prices
   c. A decrease in world oil prices
   d. An increase in investment spending
   e. An increase in taxes

9. The long-run aggregate supply curve tells us that, in the long run,
   a. the higher the price level, the higher the level of output.
   b. the higher the level of output, the higher the interest rate.
   c. the greater the money supply, the lower the interest rate.
   d. demand shocks can affect the level of output, but not the price level.
   e. demand shocks can change the price level, but not the level of output.

10. In the short run, a negative supply shock—with no change in fiscal or monetary policy—will cause
   a. the price level to rise.
   b. output to fall.
   c. the interest rate to rise.
   d. all of the above.
   e. none of the above.

True/False: For each of the following statements, circle T if the statement is true or F if the statement is false.

T   F   1. As we move rightward along the AD curve, output rises, firms units costs increase, and the price level rises.

T   F   2. According to the aggregate demand curve, a rise in the price level causes a decrease in equilibrium real GDP.

T   F   3. In the *short* run, a positive demand shock causes a rise in both the price level and real GDP.

T   F   4. In the *long* run, a positive demand shock causes a rise in the price level, but no change in output.

T   F   5. As the self-correcting mechanism brings the economy back to full employment after a positive demand shock, the average nominal wage in the economy falls.

T   F   6. Stagflation occurs as part of the economy's self-correcting mechanism after a negative demand shock.

T   F   7. The economy's aggregate supply curve can be obtained by summing up the supply curves for all the different products in the economy.

T   F   8. If we wait long enough after a negative supply shock, the average nominal wage will fall and the economy will self correct back to full employment.

CHAPTER 14

INFLATION AND MONETARY POLICY

SPEAKING ECONOMICS

Fill in each blank with the appropriate word or phrase from the list provided in the word bank. (For a challenge, fill in as many blanks as you can *without* using the word bank.)

_____ 1. The unemployment rate when there is no cyclical unemployment.

_____ 2. When the Fed keeps the money supply constant regardless of shocks to the economy.

_____ 3. When the Fed changes the money supply in response to events in the economy in order to achieve some objective.

_____ 4. The interest rate the Federal Reserve aims to achieve by adjusting the money supply.

_____ 5. A curve indicating possible combinations of inflation and unemployment in the short run.

_____ 6. A vertical line indicating that in the long run, unemployment must equal its natural rate, regardless of the rate of inflation.

Word Bank

active monetary policy   natural rate of unemployment
interest rate target   passive monetary policy
long-run Phillips curve   Phillips curve

CHAPTER HIGHLIGHTS

Fill in the blanks with the appropriate words or phrases. If you have difficulty, review the chapter and then try again.

1. When the unemployment rate is below the natural rate, GDP is _____ than potential output. The economy's self-correcting mechanism will then create inflation. When the unemployment rate is above the natural rate, GDP is _____

than potential output. The self-correcting mechanism will then put downward pressure on the price level.

2. To deal with money demand shocks, the Fed sets an interest rate target and changes the _____ as needed to maintain the target. In this way, the Fed can achieve its goals of _____ stability and full employment simultaneously.

3. To maintain full employment and _____ stability after a spending shock, the Fed must change its interest rate target. A positive spending shock requires a(n) _____ in the target; a negative spending shock requires a(n) _____ in the target.

4. When the Fed raises its interest rate target, stock and bond prices tend to _____; when it lowers its target, stock and bond prices tend to _____.

5. Good news about the economy sometimes leads to expectations that the Fed—fearing inflation—will _____ its interest rate target. This is why good economic news sometimes causes stock and bond prices to _____ . Similarly, bad news about the economy sometimes leads to expectations that the Fed—fearing recession— will _____ its interest rate target. This is why bad economic news sometimes causes stock and bond prices to _____ .

6. A negative supply shock presents the Fed with a short-run trade-off: it can limit the recession, but only at the cost of _____; and it can limit _____, but only at the cost of a deeper recession.

7. In response to a supply shock, inflation hawks lean more toward controlling _____, at the cost of greater _____. Inflation doves lean more toward limiting _____, at the cost of higher _____.

8. When inflation continues for some time, the public develops _____ that the inflation rate in the future will be similar to the inflation rate in the recent past. A continuing, stable rate of inflation gets built into the economy. The built-in rate is usually the rate that has existed for the past few years.

9. In an economy with built-in inflation, the AS curve will shift _____ each year, even when output is at full employment and unemployment is at its natural rate. The _____ shift of the AS curve will equal the built-in rate of inflation.

10. In the short run, the Fed can bring down the rate of inflation by reducing the rightward shift of the _____ curve, but only at the cost of creating a _____.

11. To neutralize a positive spending shock when there is built-in inflation, the Fed should _____ the interest rate target. This policy can maintain full employment, while keeping the rate of inflation equal to the built-in rate.

12. With built-in inflation, a negative supply shock causes a recession combined with a rise in the _____ rate. A _____ policy will lean toward reducing inflation at the cost of deepening the recession. A _____ policy will lean toward a milder recession, increasing the inflation rate.

13. The Phillips curve illustrates the economy's possible combinations of inflation and _____ in the short run, for a given built-in _____ rate.

14. In the short run, the Fed can move along the Phillips curve by adjusting the rate at which the _____ curve shifts rightward. When the Fed moves the economy downward and rightward along the Phillips curve, the _____ rate increases, and the _____ rate decreases.

15. In the long run, a decrease in the actual inflation rate leads to a lower built-in inflation rate, and the Phillips curve shifts _____.

16. In the short run, there is a tradeoff between inflation and _____: The Fed can choose lower _____ at the cost of higher inflation, or lower inflation at the cost of higher _____. But in the long run, since _____ always returns to its natural rate, there is no such tradeoff.

17. In the long run, monetary policy can change the rate of _____, but not the rate of _____.

18. The long-run Phillips curve is a _____ line at the natural rate of unemployment. The Fed can select any point along this line in the long run by using monetary policy to speed or slow the rate at which the _____ curve shifts rightward.

19. The Fed has tolerated measured inflation at 3 to 4 percent per year (1) because it knows that the _____ rate of inflation is lower; (2) because low rates of inflation may help _____ markets adjust more easily, and (3) because there is not much payoff to lowering inflation further.

IMPORTANT CONCEPTS

Write a brief answer below each of the following items.

1. In the table below, assume the economy begins at full employment. Indicate whether the Fed should *increase, decrease,* or make *no change* in the money supply in response to each event. Your answers will depend on the Fed's goal (to prevent any change in *real GDP* in the second column, and to prevent any change in the *price level* in the third column).

Event:	Change in money supply needed to stabilize real GDP	Change in money supply needed to stabilize the price level
The money demand curve shifts rightward	_____	_____
Investment decreases due to business pessimism	_____	_____
The government cuts taxes	_____	_____
World oil prices increase	_____	_____

2. Suppose that the government cuts taxes and the Fed uses an active monetary policy to prevent any change in real GDP. State what will happen to each of the following by writing *increase, decrease* or *no change.*

   a. the money supply _____

   b. the interest rate _____

   c. the price level _____

   d. investment spending _____

3. Explain what happens to each of the following from one period to the next, in a long-run equilibrium with ongoing inflation.

   a. the AD curve _____

   b. the AS curve _____

   c. real GDP _____

   d. the money supply _____

   e. the expected rate of inflation _____

4. Briefly explain how you would illustrate an increase in inflationary expectations using the Phillips curve.

5. What is the key difference between "hawk" and "dove" monetary policies? Do hawks and doves differ in policies after a demand shock, a supply shock, or both? Explain briefly.

6. Suppose the Fed wants to keep real GDP as high as possible without increasing the rate of inflation. In which of the following cases would the Fed want to maintain an unchanged interest rate target? (Write *unchanged target*.) In which cases would it want to change its interest rate target? (Write *raise target* or *lower target*.)

   a. The money demand curve shifts rightward _____

   b. Government purchases increase _____

   c. Households increase their desire to save _____

SKILLS AND TOOLS

For each of the following items, follow the instructions, write the correct answer on the blank, or circle the correct answer.

1. You've been working at the Fed for a while now, and things seem pretty calm. Real GDP is at its full-employment level and the interest rate target is still 8%. For some time, money demand has been given by the equation

$$M^d = 1,300 - 100r$$

where M^d is the quantity of money demanded (in billions of dollars) and r is the interest rate in percentage points. You check the figures from yesterday, and, sure enough, the money supply is right where it needs to be to meet the interest rate target.

   a. On the grid provided, draw the money demand curve. Also draw in the money supply curve, assuming the Fed has met its interest rate target of 8 percent. What is the money supply? _____ billion

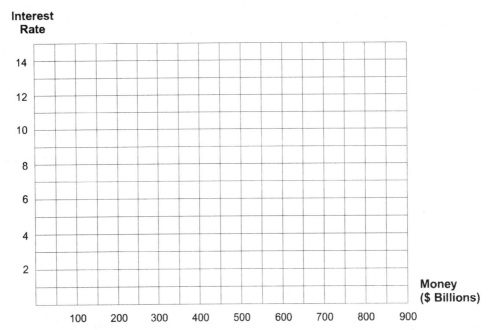

b. At 11:25 a.m. you get a buzz from the boss: New data suggest that money demand has changed to

$$M^d = 1{,}600 - 100r.$$

Draw in this new money demand curve.

c. As 11:30 a.m. draws nearer, you can see all too clearly just what will happen if nothing is done. In the money market, the interest rate will (rise/be unaffected/fall). This will (increase/have no effect on/decrease) interest-sensitive spending, and the aggregate demand (*AD*) curve will then (shift leftward/remain stable/shift rightward). Real GDP will then (rise/fall) and the economy will enter a (boom/period of calm/recession). To keep real GDP at its full employment level, you know you have to stick to your interest rate target. But to keep the interest rate at 8 percent, the money supply will have to be (increased/decreased) to a level of _____ billion. You illustrate this on your graph, and label it M^S_2.

d. You grab the phone: You've got to get through to the people in New York before 11:30 to tell them what to do. Ring after ring. Ring after ring. Where are they? What's going on up there? Can't they see what's happening? Finally a voice: "Yeah?" You scream into the mouthpiece: ("Sell bonds! Sell bonds!"/"Buy bonds! Buy bonds!"). "We've got to (increase/decrease) the money supply!" They read you loud and clear. "How much? How much?" they want to know. You check your graph and give them the answer: "I want you to (increase/decrease) the money supply by _____ billion—and I mean now!" you shout. They know, just like you know, that the demand deposit multiplier is 2.5, so they can take it from here. You head back to your desk, confident that, before long, the team in New York will be (buying/selling) bonds in the amount of _____ billion, the money supply will (increase/decrease) to _____ billion, and the interest rate will be back on target at 8 percent.

2. Life's been good after the way you handled that money demand thing. Kudos from everyone. Big promotion, too: Now they've got *you* making some of the decisions, and *someone else* making the graphs for *you*. Things are pretty good.

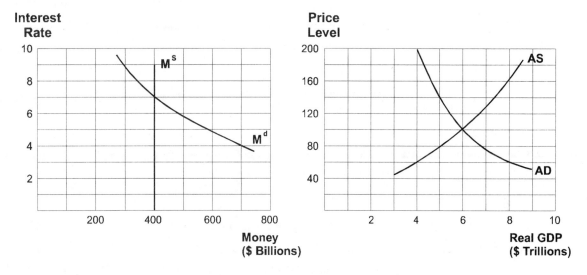

a. Over your (now usual) morning latte, you check the morning's graphs, above: the money supply is at _____ billion and the equilibrium interest rate is _____ percent. Since the interest rate target is 7 percent, the interest rate is (a bit too high/right on target/a bit too low). Real GDP is at its full-employment level of _____ trillion, and the price level is at _____.

b. You kick back and pick up your copy of *The Wall Street Journal*—and there's the screaming headline: *Investment Spending Plummets as Big Business Gets Bad Case of Jitters!* What does it mean? What does it mean? You know they'll all come running down to ask you any minute now. You reach for *Hall & Lieberman*. Now you remember: an unexpected decline in investment spending is a (positive/negative) spending shock. This will shift aggregate demand (rightward/leftward), causing both the price level and real GDP to (rise/fall). This, in turn, will cause the money demand curve to shift (rightward/leftward).

c. If the Fed does nothing, you've got a pretty good idea that *AD* will shift by $2 trillion at every price level, and money demand will shift by $200 billion at every level of the interest rate. There's no time to wait for your assistant—you've got to plot the new *AD* and money demand curves yourself—so do it now!

d. If these shifts occur, we'd then be looking at short run equilibrium real GDP of _____ billion which would be (above/below) the full-employment level, and an equilibrium price level of _____. We'd also be looking at an equilibrium interest rate of _____ which is (above/below) the target of 7 percent.

e. Once you get a chance to think things over, you see that a passive policy is not the way to go. Besides the short run impact on prices, the interest rate, and real GDP described in part (c), there is also the long run to consider. In the long run, doing nothing means the economy will slide along the (original *AS* curve/new *AD* curve), and output will return to its full employment level, but the price level will (fall further/rise back) to the level of _____. Of course, the Fed could instead stick to its interest rate target of 7%. To do this, the Fed will have to counter the decrease in investment with a(n) (increase/decrease) in the money supply, pushing the interest rate (up/down) to 7% and, as a result, causing interest-sensitive consumption and investment spending to (rise/fall). This would only shift the *AD* curve (leftward/rightward) from the one graphed in part (c), so this would clearly (be the best policy/*not* be the best policy).

f. The only option you haven't considered would be to change the interest rate target itself. If the Fed did that, it would want to set a target (above/below) its original 7%, and indeed set it even (lower/higher) than the equilibrium in part (c). To do that, the Fed would have to (increase/decrease) the money supply. The resulting (increase/decrease) in the interest rate would cause interest sensitive spending to (increase/decrease) and the economy could be made to (return to full employment GDP and a price level of 100/fall deeper into recession and deflation).

g. Here they come. What are you going to recommend? Should the Fed: (1) follow a passive policy, (2) maintain the interest rate target of 7 percent, or (3) change the target? (1 / 2 / 3).

3. It was Monday, January 23. It was cold in Washington. We were working the night watch out of Price Level. The boss is Alan Greenspan. My partner is Bill Cannon. My name is Phillips.

For the last few years the unemployment rate had been what everyone calls the natural rate: 5.5 percent—though how it could be "natural" when people were still out of work was beyond me, but that's another story. Right now we were looking at inflation, and inflation had been running pretty high in this town; 14 percent, year after year, and people had just gotten used to it. Everyone thought it just had to be that way. Everyone but me and my partner, that is.

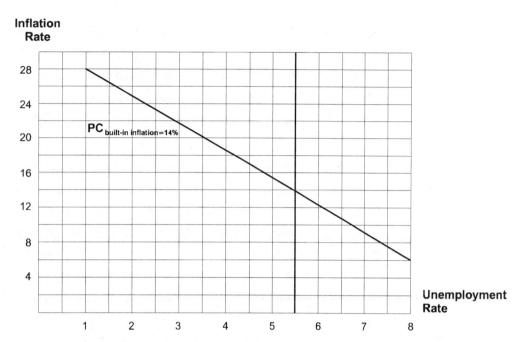

a. "New inflation and unemployment rates are in, Joe."

"Uh-huh."

"Inflation's hit 22%"

"That right?"

"But look at this unemployment rate, Joe."

"I don't need to look at it Bill. I can read the curve. If inflation just hit 22 percent, unemployment must be approximately _____ percent."

b. "Must have been some kind of a shock, Joe."

"Uh-huh."

"What d'ya think, Joe: Demand shock? Supply shock?"

"With inflation rising and unemployment falling, it's got to have been a (demand/supply) shock now, doesn't it? And a (negative/positive) one at that."

c. "What's gonna happen, Joe?"

"Well, that all depends what the boys upstairs do now, doesn't it? If they hold the actual inflation rate at 22 percent like this for year after year, well, then expectations will change and the built-in rate of inflation will (rise/fall) to _____ percent, and the *PC* curve is going to shift (upward/downward), now won't it? In the long run, we could then look forward to continuing inflation of 22 percent and an unemployment rate of _____ percent. On the other hand, they could step right up and counter the shock, and force the inflation rate back down to 14 percent. That way the *PC* curve won't shift."

d. "Is that what you'd do Joe? You'd push inflation back down to 14 percent?"

"Is that what I'd do? No, that's not what I'd do. I'll tell you what I'd do: I'd force inflation all the way down to 8 percent, and I'd do it right now."

"But Joe, if inflation is forced down to 8 percent, in the short run we'll move (down/up) the $PC_{\text{built-in inflation} = 14\%}$ curve and the unemployment rate will (rise/fall) to approximately _____ percent."

"Yeah. But in the long run, if we can keep the actual inflation rate down to 8 percent, expectations will change and the built-in inflation rate will eventually become _____ percent, and the PC curve will shift (downward/upward) _____. When it does, we'll be able to have a lower inflation rate of 8 percent and a (lower/higher) unemployment rate of _____ percent.

"That's pretty tough medicine, Joe."

"Its tough medicine, alright, but inflation's a tough character."

"You really hate inflation, don't you Joe?"

"Hate inflation? You bet I hate inflation. Inflation's a thief, Bill. It comes in the night—every night—and it robs old ladies on fixed pensions of all their purchasing power. That's not my idea of something to like, Bill. Call me old fashioned but that's how I feel."

"Its morning Joe. The day watch just came in. Let's go home."

15-MINUTE PRACTICE TEST

Set a timer, giving yourself just 15 minutes to answer all of the following questions. To see what you *really* know and remember, take the test at least a day *after* you've read the chapter in the text and completed the exercises in this study guide.

Multiple Choice: Circle the letter in front of the single best answer.

1. In recent years, the Fed has
   a. followed a passive monetary policy.
   b. followed an active monetary policy.
   c. been confused and indecisive in its policy-making.
   d. successfully stabilized real GDP, but worsened inflation.
   e. successfully maintained low inflation, but at the cost of many severe recessions.

2. If the Fed wants to prevent any change in real GDP when the money demand curve shifts rightward, it should
   a. pursue an active monetary policy.
   b. maintain its interest rate target.
   c. increase the money supply.
   d. all of the above.
   e. none of the above.

3. When the Fed raises its interest rate target,

    a. the inflation rate usually rises.
    b. real GDP usually rises.
    c. investment spending usually rises.
    d. consumption spending usually rises.
    e. stock and bond prices usually fall.

4. If the Fed pursues a passive monetary policy, a negative supply shock will cause

    a. the price level to fall.
    b. real GDP to rise.
    c. the economy to experience stagflation.
    d. all of the above.
    e. none of the above.

5. When the economy experiences a negative supply shock, and the Fed follows a relatively "dovish" monetary policy, we can expect

    a. relatively greater increases in the price level (or greater increases in the inflation rate).
    b. relatively greater increases in the unemployment rate.
    c. relatively greater decreases in the price level (or greater decreases in the inflation rate).
    d. relatively greater decreases in the unemployment rate.
    e. no change in the price level, in the inflation rate, or the unemployment rate.

6. Fill in the blank: During a negative supply shock, a "hawk" monetary policy will result in a smaller rise in _____ than would a "dove" monetary policy.

    a. the price level
    b. output
    c. unemployment
    d. all of the above
    e. b and c only

7. A rise in the expected inflation rate causes

    a. the AD curve to shift leftward.
    b. the AS curve to shift downward.
    c. the Phillips curve to shift upward.
    d. a movement rightward along the Phillips curve.
    e. a movement leftward along the Phillips curve.

8. If the Fed begins shifting the AD curve rightward at a faster rate than in the past, the short-run effect is a

    a. movement rightward along the Phillips curve.
    b. movement leftward along the Phillips curve.
    c. downward shift of the Phillips curve.
    d. leftward shift of the AD curve.
    e. downward shift of the AS curve.

9. One harmful consequence of using monetary policy to lower the rate of unemployment below its natural rate is that it causes

    a. a movement rightward along the Phillips curve in the long run.
    b. an upward shift in the Phillips curve in the long run.
    c. a decrease in transfer payments in the short run.
    d. an increase in tax revenue in the short run.
    e. inefficient businesses to survive and prosper since the economy is performing "too well."

10. One reason that the Fed does *not* reduce inflation all the way to zero is that

    a. the Fed does not know how to reduce the inflation rate below one or two percent per year.
    b. Federal law forbids the Fed from reducing the inflation rate to zero.
    c. the Fed fears a "rebound" effect, in which the inflation rate would bounce back up to even higher levels than before the reduction.
    d. the benefits of reducing inflation all the way to zero are too low to justify the costs to society.
    e. the official inflation rate underestimates the true inflation rate, so if the Fed reduced the true rate to zero, the official rate would be negative.

True/False: For each of the following statements, circle T if the statement is true or F if the statement is false.

T   F   1. When the unemployment rate falls below the natural rate, real GDP falls below potential output.

T   F   2. Under a passive monetary policy, a rightward shift of the money demand curve will cause a leftward shift of the AD curve.

T   F   3. Under an active monetary policy designed to stabilize real GDP, a rightward shift of the money demand curve will cause the Fed to raise its interest rate target.

T   F   4. To stabilize real GDP, the Fed should respond to a spending shock with a passive monetary policy.

T   F   5. When the Fed raises its interest rate target, bond prices tend to fall and stock prices tend to rise.

T   F   6. A negative demand shock presents the Fed with a short-run tradeoff: it must choose between higher inflation or higher unemployment.

T   F   7. In the long run, the economy's self-correcting mechanism returns the economy back to full employment after a demand shock, but not after a supply shock.

T   F   8. In an economy with built in inflation, the AS curve will shift up each year, even when output is at full employment and unemployment is at its natural rate.

CHAPTER 15

FISCAL POLICY: TAXES, SPENDING, AND THE FEDERAL BUDGET

CHAPTER HIGHLIGHTS

Fill in the blanks with the appropriate words or phrases. If you have difficulty, review the chapter and then try again.

1. When examining budget-related figures over time, it is grossly misleading to use _____ figures, since the price level rises over time.

2. Budget-related figures such as government spending or the national debt have meaning only when considered relative to a nation's total _____. This is why we should always look at these figures as percentages of _____.

3. Viewed as a percentage of _____, non-military government purchases have remained low and stable. They have not contributed to growth in total government spending.

4. Viewed as a percentage of _____, military purchases have _____ dramatically over the past several decades. Like non-military purchases, they have not contributed to any growth in government spending.

5. The decline in _____ spending in relation to GDP since the early 1960s has made huge amounts of resources available for other purposes. But because _____ spending is now only 4 percent of GDP and probably cannot drop much further, there cannot be any similar freeing up of resources in coming decades.

6. In recent decades, _____ has (have) been the fastest growing part of federal government spending and are currently equal to about 8 percent of GDP.

7. Over the past several decades, and until the early 1990s, federal government spending as a percentage of GDP rose steadily. The main causes were increases in _____ payments and increases in _____ on the national debt.

8. From 1992 to 1999, federal government spending as a percentage of GDP _____ steadily, although it remained a _____ percentage than in 1950. The main causes have been the continued sharp _____ in military spending, and more modest _____ in transfer payments relative to GDP.

9. Federal revenue has trended _____ from around 17 percent of GDP in 1959 to around _____ percent in 1999.

10. _____—which add to the public's holdings of government bonds—add to the national debt. _____—which decrease the public's bond holdings—subtract from the national debt.

11. In a recession, because _____ rise(s) and _____ fall(s), the federal budget deficit rises. In a boom, because _____ decrease(s) and _____ rise(s), the budget deficit falls.

12. Many features of the federal tax and transfer systems act as automatic
    _____. As the economy goes into a recession, these features help to
    _____ the decline in consumption spending, and they also cause the
    cyclical deficit to rise. As the economy goes into boom, these features help to
    _____ the rise in consumption spending, and they also cause the cyclical
    deficit to fall.

13. As long as the national debt grows by the same percentage as _____ , the
    ratios of debt to _____ and interest payments to _____
    will remain constant. in this case, the government can continue to pay interest on its rising
    debt without increasing the average tax rate in the economy.

14. Macroeconomists prefer to look at the _____ budget surplus or deficit—
    the difference between the government's total tax revenue (including
    _____ taxes) and its total spending (including _____
    benefits).

15. Part of the recent expansion has been associated with a rapid rise in
    _____ GDP, caused by rapid technological change. Technological
    change—which has increased the _____ of the U.S. labor force much
    faster than previously—has led to more rapid growth in our capacity to produce goods and
    services.

16. Another reason for the recent change from budget deficit to budget surplus is cyclical: with
    each passing year since 1991, the economy has operated closer and closer it its
    _____ output and—in the late 1990s—output may even have exceeded
    its _____ level.

IMPORTANT CONCEPTS

Write a brief answer below each of the following items.

1. List the three broad categories of the federal government's spending.

   a.

   b.

   c.

2. Briefly, what is the difference between federal government *purchases* and federal government *spending*?

3. State whether each of the following has experienced an *upward trend*, *downward trend*, or *remained steady* over the past few decades.

   a. transfer payments as a percentage of GDP _____

   b. total federal government *purchases* as a percentage of GDP _____

   c. total federal government *spending* as a percentage of GDP _____

   d. social security tax revenue as a percentage of GDP _____

   e. total federal tax revenue as a percentage of GDP _____

4. List three reasons why economists recommend against the use of countercyclical fiscal policy.

   a.

   b.

   c.

SKILLS AND TOOLS

For each of the following items, follow the instructions, write the correct answer in the blank, or circle the correct answer.

1. The table below reports data on the U.S. economy from 1982 to 1999. The figures are in billions of current dollars.

Year	GDP	Military Government Purchases	Non-military Government Purchases	Military Government Purchases as a Percentage of GDP	Non-military Government Purchases as a Percentage of GDP	Total Government Purchases as a Percentage of GDP
1982	$3,259.2	$228.3	$84.5	7.00	_____	9.60
1983	$3,534.9	$252.5	$92.0	_____	2.60	9.75
1984	$3,932.7	$283.5	$92.8	7.21	2.36	9.57
1985	$4,213.0	$312.4	$101.0	_____	_____	_____
1986	$4,452.9	$332.2	$106.5	7.46	2.39	9.85
1987	$4,742.5	$351.2	$109.3	_____	2.30	_____
1988	$5,108.3	$355.9	$106.8	6.97	_____	9.06
1989	$5,489.1	$363.2	$119.3	6.62	2.17	_____
1990	$5,803.2	$374.9	$133.6	_____	_____	8.76
1991	$5,986.2	$384.5	$142.9	6.42	2.39	8.81
1992	$6,318.9	$378.5	$156.0	_____	2.47	_____
1993	$6,642.3	$364.9	$162.4	5.49	_____	7.94
1994	$7,054.3	$355.1	$165.9	5.03	2.35	_____
1995	$7,400.5	$350.6	$170.9	4.74	_____	7.05
1996	$7,813.2	$357.0	$174.6	_____	2.23	_____
1997	$8,300.8	$352.5	$185.3	4.25	2.23	6.48
1998	$8,759.9	$348.6	$190.1	3.98	_____	6.15
1999	$9,256.1	$364.5	$206.1	_____	2.23	6.16

a. By glancing down the column for non-military government purchases, we can see that, except between 1987 and 1988, this component of government purchases (increased/remained steady/decreased) in nominal terms every single year. In fact, between 1982 and 1999, this component of government spending (more than doubled/kept steady/fell by half). Looking at this, alone, may we conclude that non-military government purchases are a rapidly growing burden on the American economy?

(Yes/No). To properly gauge levels and trends in budget-related expenditures, one must always consider (nominal values/absolute real values/the spending as a percent of GDP).

b. Complete the entries in the table. Then, using figures from the table, plot and label military purchases as a percentage of GDP, non-military purchases as a percentage of GDP, and total government purchases as a percentage of GDP on the grid below.

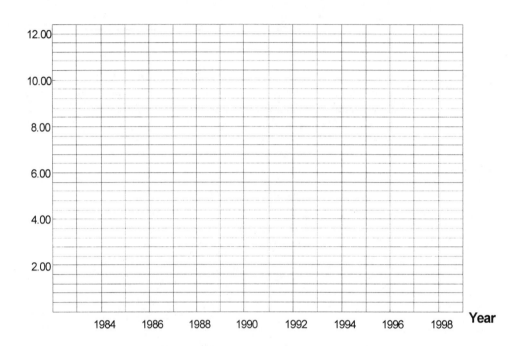

c. Viewed as a percentage of GDP, non-military government purchases (are low and stable/are high and stable/vary wildly). Indeed, between 1982 to 1999, this component of total government spending actually (increased/decreased) as a percentage of GDP, from a level of _____ percent in 1982 to a level of _____ percent in 1999.

d. Viewed as a percentage of GDP, military government purchases have steadily decreased since _____. Over the entire period 1982 to 1999, this component of total government spending reached its peak of _____ percent of GDP in the year _____, and fell to its lowest level of _____ percent in the year _____.

e. From 1982 to 1986, total government purchases as a percentage of GDP (increased/decreased) from a level of _____ to a level of _____. From their peak _____ percent in the year _____, these expenditures as a percentage of GDP (increased/decreased) rather steadily, ending the period in 1999 at a level of _____ percent of GDP.

2.   Remember the economy of Upper Classica? The supply of loanable funds from all sources there is given by the equation

$$F^S = (r-1)/2,$$

where r is the interest rate measured in percentage points (e.g. seven percent is 7 rather than decimal 0.07). For some time now the government has been spending no more than it collects in taxes, so Upper Classica has enjoyed a period with no deficits or surpluses in the government budget. As a result, total demand for loanable funds in Upper Classica has been stable and given by the equation,

$$F^D = (7-r)/2,$$

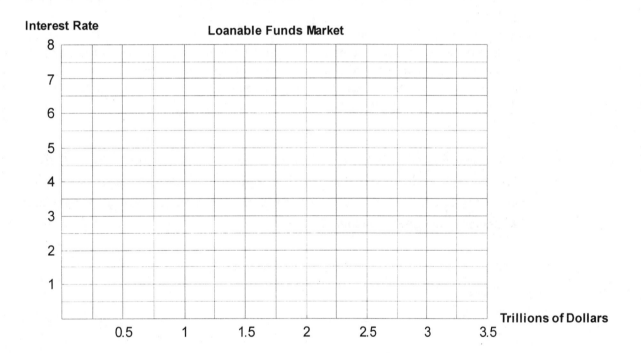

a.   Graph the total demand for funds and the total supply of funds in the grid provided.

b.   When the government of Upper Classica runs neither a budget deficit nor a budget surplus, the equilibrium interest rate is _____ percent and the quantity of funds demanded and supplied is _____ trillion dollars.

It is an election year in Upper Classica and two very attractive candidates have stepped forward, each with a different vision of the country's long run economic future. One candidate favors holding the line on taxes and increasing government spending; the other candidate also favors holding the line on taxes, but wants to reduce government spending, not increase it

c. If the candidate favoring increased government spending were to be elected, and his program enacted, the government of Upper Classica would begin to run budget deficits. If this deficit were to be equal to one (1) trillion dollars per year, then the (demand for/supply of) funds would shift (leftward/rightward) by (less than one trillion/exactly one trillion/more than one trillion) dollars at every level of the interest rate. Draw in that newly shifted curve on the grid above. We can see that this candidate's proposed program of continuing deficits will lead to (a higher/ an unchanged/ a lower) equilibrium interest rate of _____ percent.

d. If the candidate favoring decreased government spending were to be elected, and her program enacted, the government of Upper Classica would begin to run budget surpluses. If this surplus were to be equal to one-half (0.5) trillion dollars per year, then the (demand for/supply of) funds would shift (leftward/rightward) by (less than one-half trillion/exactly one-half trillion/more than one-half trillion) dollars at every level of the interest rate. Draw in that newly shifted curve on the grid above. We can see that this candidate's proposed program of continuing surpluses will lead to (a higher/ an unchanged/ a lower) equilibrium interest rate of _____ percent.

3.   In the debates last night, the candidates in Upper Classica's election hammered each other over the impact their rival economic plans would have on the average standard of living. The candidate favoring deficits even brought along the graph, below, showing Upper Classica's aggregate production function.

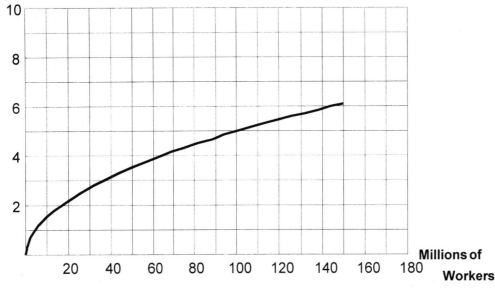

a.   Both candidates agreed on how the government's budget affects the aggregate production function, and so average standards of living. Both agreed that by affecting interest rates, the government budget deficit or surplus affects (the money supply/ investment spending) which, in turn, affects the rate of growth of (the stock of bonds/ the stock of capital). Even with no change in economic policy, both agreed that the aggregate production function tends to (shift up/ stay unchanged / shift downward) over time— where they said their policies differed was in how rapidly those shifts would occur.

b.   The candidate favoring surpluses argued that her policy, by (increasing /holding constant /decreasing) the (demand for/ supply of) loanable funds, and so forcing the equilibrium interest rate (down/to remain steady/up), would encourage (a greater increase/ no change/ a smaller increase) in investment spending and so tend to shift the aggregate production function (upward/downward) at a (slower/faster) rate. This, of course, would lead to (more rapid/less rapid) improvement in the average standard of living, compared to the status quo.

c.   The candidate favoring deficits had to admit that his policy, by (increasing /holding constant /decreasing) the (demand for/ supply of) loanable funds, and so forcing the equilibrium interest rate (down/to remain steady/up), would encourage (a greater increase/ no change/ a smaller increase) in investment spending and so tend to shift the aggregate production function (upward/downward) at a (slower/faster) rate. This, of course, would lead to (more rapid/less rapid) improvement in the average standard of living, compared to the status quo.

4.   During the last half hour of their debate, the candidates finally got around to discussing how their rival policies would affect the national debt. No one really cared much about all that until one of the candidates pointed out that continuing deficits in the government budget will cause the national debt to rise. This, in turn, would eventually require the government to reduce spending or increase taxes in order to continue paying the rising interest bill. Just the mere mention of "taxes" seemed to galvanize the audience. The moderator of the debate quickly noted that taxes can affect incentives to work, and asked each candidate to explain how his or her plan would affect the national labor market equilibrium, depicted below.

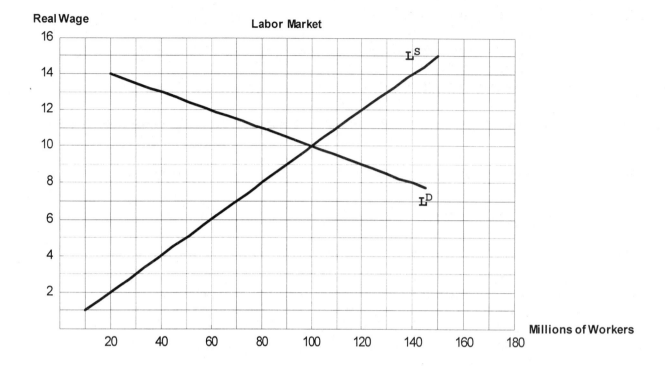

a.   The candidate favoring deficits had to answer first. He admitted that the (higher/lower)
     taxes that might eventually be necessary under his plan would (encourage/discourage)
     work, and so tend to shift the (demand for/ supply of) labor (rightward/leftward). Since he
     said he estimated the size of this shift at no more than 30 million workers at each level of
     the real wage, he confidently predicted that if his plan were enacted the equilibrium real
     wage would (rise/fall) to _____ from its current level of 10.

b.   To close the debate, the candidate favoring surpluses stepped forward to answer. She
     declared that the (higher/lower) taxes that might eventually be possible under her plan
     would (encourage/discourage) work, and so tend to shift the (demand for/ supply of) labor
     (rightward/leftward). Since she said she estimated the size of this shift at no more than 30
     million workers at each level of the real wage, she admitted that if her plan were enacted
     the equilibrium real wage would (rise/fall) to _____ from its current level
     of 10.

15-MINUTE PRACTICE TEST

Set a timer, giving yourself just 15 minutes to answer all of the following questions. To see what you *really* know and remember, take the test at least a day *after* you've read the chapter in the text and completed the exercises in this study guide.

Multiple Choice: Circle the letter in front of the single best answer.

1. When observing how the federal budget has changed over time, it is best to look at how the budget figures have changed

   a. in nominal terms.
   b. in real terms.
   c. as a percentage of GDP.
   d. as a percentage of the national debt.
   e. as a percentage of the budget deficit.

2. Which of the following has declined dramatically in recent decades?

   a. Nominal military spending
   b. Real military spending
   c. Military spending as a percentage of GDP
   d. Real non-military spending
   e. Non-military spending as a percentage of GDP

3. Which of the following has trended upward as a percentage of GDP in recent decades?

   a. Federal transfer payments
   b. Federal government spending
   c. Social security tax revenue
   d. All of the above
   e. None of the above

4. Total federal tax revenue as a percentage of GDP has, in recent decades,

   a. risen dramatically.
   b. fallen dramatically.
   c. remained constant at about 50%.
   d. trended upward slightly, from around 17% to around 20%.
   e. trended upward slightly, from around 2% to around 3%.

5. Which of the following would cause the national debt to rise as a fraction of real GDP?

   a. Any budget deficit greater than zero
   b. Any cyclical budget deficit greater than zero
   c. Any structural budget deficit greater than zero
   d. Only budget deficits greater than about 3% of GDP
   e. Only budget deficits greater than about 10% of real GDP

6. When the federal government runs a budget surplus,

    a. the surplus is equal to the budget deficit.
    b. the national debt decreases..
    c. the government must borrow the surplus in the loanable funds market.
    d. it sells government bonds to the public.
    e. all of the above.

7. In a recession,

    a. tax revenues fall.
    b. transfer payments rise.
    c. the cyclical deficit rises.
    d. all of the above.
    e. none of the above.

8. The structural deficit is the part of the deficit that

    a. rises and falls in recessions and booms.
    b. is due to wasteful, as opposed to useful, government spending.
    c. is due to useful, as opposed to wasteful, government spending.
    d. is due to spending on infrastructure, like roads and bridges.
    e. none of the above.

9. Which of the following acts as an automatic stabilizer in the economy?

    a. Unemployment insurance
    b. Welfare payments
    c. Income taxes
    d. All of the above
    e. None of the above

10. Which of the following is an important explanation for why the budget has gone into surplus in the late 1990s?

    a. Changes in the measurement of GDP.
    b. rapid technological change.
    c. higher inflation.
    d. all of the above.
    e. none of the above.

True/False: For each of the following statements, circle T if the statement is true or F if the statement is false.

T   F   1. Viewed as a percentage of GDP, total government purchases have remained steady over the past several decades.

T   F   2. Viewed as a percentage of GDP, military spending has trended downward over the past several decades.

T   F   3. A federal budget deficit of any size causes the national debt to rise.

T   F   4. A federal budget deficit of any size causes the national debt as a percentage of GDP to rise.

T   F   5. Economists today believe that countercyclical fiscal policy can be as effective as countercyclical monetary policy in stabilizing the economy.

T   F   6. The structural budget deficit is the part of the deficit that is not affected by booms and recessions.

T   F   7. In the long run, an increase in transfer payments—with no other fiscal change—can be expected to lead to slower growth in the average standard of living.

T   F   8. Both historical experience and economic theory suggest that the United States was on the brink of a "debt disaster" in the 1980s, and that financial collapse was imminent.

CHAPTER 16

EXCHANGE RATES AND MACROECONOMIC POLICY

Fill in each blank with the appropriate word or phrase from the list provided in the word bank. (For a challenge, fill in as many blanks as you can *without* using the word bank.)

_____ 1. The market in which one country's currency is traded for another country's.

_____ 2. The amount of one country's currency that is traded for one unit of another country's currency.

_____ 3. A curve indicating the quantity of a specific foreign currency that Americans will want to buy, during a given period, at each different exchange rate.

_____ 4. A curve indicating the quantity of a specific foreign currency that will be supplied during a given period, at each different exchange rate.

_____ 5. An exchange rate that is freely determined by the forces of supply and demand.

_____ 6. An increase in the price of a currency in a floating-rate system.

_____ 7. A decrease in the price of a currency in a floating-rate system.

_____ 8. The idea that the exchange rate will adjust in the long run so that the average price of goods in two countries will be roughly the same.

_____ 9. Simultaneous buying and selling of a foreign currency in order to profit from a difference in exchange rates.

_____ 10. Arbitrage involving one pair of currencies.

_____ 11. Arbitrage involving trades among three (or more) currencies.

_____ 12. A policy of frequent central bank intervention to move the exchange rate.

_____ 13. A government declared exchange rate maintainted by central bank intervention in the foreign excange market.

_____ 14. A change in the exchange rate form a higher fixed rate to a lower fixed rate.

_____ 15. A loss of faith that a country can prevent a drop in its exchange rate, leading to a rapid depletion of its foreign currency (e.g. dollar) reserves.

_____ 16. A region whose economies perform better with a single currency than with separate national currencies.

_____ 17. The excess of a nation's imports over its exports during a given period.

_____ 18. The excess of a nation's exports over its imports during a given period.

_____ 19. An inflow of funds equal to a nation's trade deficit.

Word Bank

appreciation	foreign exchange market
arbitrage	managed float
bilateral arbitrage	net capital inflow
demand curve for foreign currency	optimum currency area
devaluation	purchasing power parity (PPP) theory
depreciation	supply curve for foreign currency
exchange rate	trade deficit
fixed exchange rate	trade surplus
floating exchange rate	triangular arbitrage
foreign currency crisis	

⟨ CHAPTER HIGHLIGHTS ⟩

Fill in the blanks with the appropriate words or phrases. If you have difficulty, review the chapter and then try again.

1. The _____ is the price of foreign currency in dollars.

2. In our model of the market for pounds, we assume that American households and businesses are the only _____ of pounds.

3. In our model of the market for pounds, we assume that British households and firms are the only _____ of pounds.

4. When the exchange rate _____—that is, when the government does not interfere in the foreign currency market—the equilibrium exchange rate is determined by the intersection of the demand curve and the supply curve.

5. When a floating exchange rate changes, one country's currency will _____ (rise in price) and the other country's currency will _____ (fall in price).

6. Relative interest rates and expectations of future exchange rates are the dominant forces moving exchange rates in the very _____ run.

7. In the _____ run, movements in exchange rates are caused largely by economic fluctuations. All else being equal, a country whose GDP rises relatively rapidly will experience a(n) _____ of its currency. A country whose GDP falls more rapidly will experience a(n) _____ of its currency.

8. According to the purchasing power _____ theory, an exchange rate between two countries will adjust in the _____ run until the average price of goods is roughly the same in both countries.

9. In the long run, the currency of a country with a higher inflation rate will _____ against the currency of a country whose inflation rate is lower.

10. _____ arbitrage ensures that the exchange rate between any two currencies is the same everywhere in the world.

11. _____ arbitrage ensures that the price of a foreign currency is the same whether it is purchased directly—in a single foreign exchange market—or indirectly, by buying and selling a third currency.

12. Under a managed float, a country's central bank buys its own currency to prevent a(n) _____, and sells its own currency to prevent a(n) _____.

13. When a country fixes its exchange rate below the equilibrium value, the result is an excess _____ for (of) the country's currency. To maintain the fixed rate, the country's central bank must _____ enough of its own currency to eliminate the excess _____ .

14. When a country fixes its exchange rate above the equilibrium value, the result is an excess
_____ for (of) the country's currency. To maintain the fixed rate, the
country's central bank must _____ enough of its own currency to
eliminate the excess _____ .

15. A foreign currency crisis arises when people no longer believe that a country can maintain a
fixed exchange rate _____ the equilibrium rate. As a consequence, the
supply of the currency _____ , demand for it _____ ,
and the country must use up its reserves of dollars and other key currencies even faster in
order to maintain the fixed rate.

16. A depreciation of the dollar causes net exports to _____ —a
_____ spending shock that _____ real GDP in the
short run. An appreciation of the dollar causes net exports to _____ —a
_____ spending shock that _____ real GDP in the
short run.

17. Monetary policy has a _____ effect when we include the impact on
exchange rates and net exports, rather than just the impact on interest-sensitive consumption
and investment spending.

18. An increase in the desire of foreigners to invest in the United States contributes to a (an)
_____ of the dollar. As a result, U.S. exports _____
because they are _____ expensive for foreigners. Imports
_____ , because they are _____ expensive to
Americans. The result is a(n) _____ in the trade deficit.

19. We can trace the rise in the U.S. trade deficit during the 1980s and 1990s to two important
sources: first, relatively high _____ in the 1980s; and second, a long
held preference for American assets that grew stronger in the 1990s. Each of these
contributed to a large capital inflow, a _____ value for the dollar, and a
trade deficit.

IMPORTANT CONCEPTS

Write a brief answer below each of the following items.

1. In the market where Mexican pesos are exchanged for U.S. dollars, list four changes that would cause the demand curve for pesos to shift *leftward*. (The text discusses five such changes for the case of the British pound.)

   a.

   b.

   c.

   d.

2. List four changes that would cause the supply curve for Mexican pesos to shift *leftward*. (The text discusses five such changes for the case of the British pound.)

   a.

   b.

   c.

   d.

3. Using the supply and demand model of the market where pounds and dollars are traded, state whether each of the following changes would cause the dollar to *appreciate*, *depreciate*, or *remain unchanged* relative to the British pound. In each case, assume that the dollar floats against the pound, and that there are no other changes that affect the exchange rate, other than the one listed.

   a. real GDP in Britain rises _____

   b. the interest rate in the United States rises _____

   c. the interest rate in Britain falls _____

   d. Americans develop a taste for British tea _____

   e. Americans and Brits expect the pound to depreciate in the near future _____

   f. the price level in Britain rises _____

4. Suppose the dollar floats against the Japanese yen, and the Fed increases the U.S. money supply. State whether each of the following variables would *increase*, *decrease*, or *remain unchanged*.

   a. real GDP in the United States _____

   b. the interest rate in the United States _____

   c. the exchange rate (dollars per yen) _____

   d. United States net exports to Japan _____

5. Suppose a country fixes its exchange rate with the dollar *above* the equilibrium exchange rate. Therefore, it must buy its own currency in the foreign exchange market to maintain the fixed rate. State whether the country would have to buy more, less, or the same amount of its own currency after each change listed below.

   a. real GDP in the country increases _____

   b. the interest rate in the country increases _____

   c. people suddenly gain confidence in the country's ability to maintain the fixed rate _____

   d. citizens of the country develop an increased taste for foreign goods _____

SKILLS AND TOOLS

For each of the following items, follow the instructions, write the correct answer in the blank, or circle the correct answer.

1. A currency table is a convenient and very common way to display exchange rate information. The table below was obtained one day in May, 1999, from *Yahoo!* at the URL http://quote.yahoo.com/m3?u

Notice that currencies are arranged in rows and columns. Looking across each row, you obtain the price of the column-currency in units of the row-currency: Looking down any column, you obtain the price of the column-currency in units of the row-currency.

Currency	US $	Aust $	UK £	Can $	DMark	FFranc	¥en	SFranc
US $	____	0.5915	____	0.6674	____	0.1358	0.009239	0.5753
Aust $	1.691	____	2.606	1.128	0.7701	0.2296	____	0.9726
UK £	0.6488	0.3838	1	0.433	____	____	0.005994	____
Can $	____	____	2.309	____	0.6825	0.2035	0.01384	0.862
DMark	2.195	1.299	3.384	1.465	____	____	0.02028	____
FFranc	7.364	____	11.35	____	3.354	____	0.06803	4.236
¥en	____	64.02	____	72.24	49.3	17.7	____	62.27
SFranc	1.783	1.028	2.679	____	0.7918	0.2361	0.01606	____

a. Fill in the blanks.

b. If a Canadian resident were planning to buy a French bond costing FF200,000, at the exchange rates prevailing on this day in May, she would have to spend _____ Canadian dollars.

c. If an American resident were planning to buy a French bond costing FF200,000, at the exchange rates prevailing on this day in May, he would have to spend _____ U.S. dollars.

d. If a Japanese resident were planning to buy American real estate costing US $1,000,000, at the exchange rates prevailing on this day in May, she would have to spend _____ Japanese Yen.

e. If an American resident were planning to buy a British automobile costing £20,000, at the exchange rates prevailing on this day in May, he would have to spend _____ U.S. dollars.

f. If a German resident were planning to buy French fertilizer costing FF50,000, at the exchange rates prevailing on this day in May, he would have to spend _____ DMarks.

2. Suppose that the United States and France are the only two countries that trade with one another. The American demand for French francs is given by

$$D^{FF} = 14 - 40e.$$

The French supply of francs is

$$S^{FF} = 30e$$

Here, D^{FF} is quantity of francs demanded, S^{FF} is quantity of francs supplied, both in hundreds of millions per day. The variable e in both equations is the exchange rate, giving the dollar price of a unit of French currency.

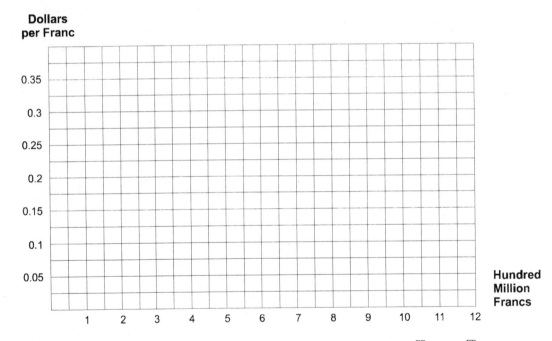

a. Plot the demand and supply curves for French francs. Label them D^{FF}_1 and S^{FF}_1.

b. At an exchange rate of $0.25, American buyers of French goods and assets will want to buy _____ hundred million French francs on the foreign exchange market. At that same price, French buyers of American goods and assets will want to sell _____ hundred million French francs. At an exchange rate of $0.25, the quantity of francs demanded will (exceed/equal/be exceeded by) the quantity of francs supplied. As a result, the French franc will tend to (appreciate/remain unchanged/depreciate) and the U.S. dollar will tend to (appreciate/remain unchanged/depreciate). The foreign exchange market is in equilibrium when the exchange rate is _____.

c. Suppose the United States experiences a sharp recession. This will cause (American demand for French francs/French supply of francs) to shift (leftward/rightward). If the amount of this shift is FF3.5 hundred million at every level of the exchange rate, what is the new equilibrium exchange rate? _____ Illustrate by drawing in the new supply or demand curve, whichever is appropriate.

d. Following the shift in part (c), and after much national soul-searching, French consumers discover that they really do love American movies after all. This change in tastes toward American products will cause (American demand for French francs/French supply of francs) to shift (leftward/rightward). If the amount of this shift is FF1.75 hundred million at every level of the exchange rate, what is the new equilibrium exchange rate? _____ Illustrate by drawing in the new supply or demand curve, whichever is appropriate.

3. Imagine you are hard at work as a currency trader in New York City. You study your computer screen and notice the following data from the most recent trades:

   Time: 11:43 a.m. Eastern Standard Time

   Place: New York Inter-Bank market

   Items:

Price of pound sterling in dollar-pound market:	$2.00
Price of French franc in dollar-franc market :	$0.05
Price of pound sterling in franc-pound market:	FF 10

Your heart starts pounding.

a. You notice that the direct price of one pound to Americans is _____. At the same time, the indirect price of one pound to Americans is _____.

   No time to lose … You've got authority to spend up to $100,000 if you see an opportunity, and you do. You start punching up the orders:

b. First, you place an order to buy (francs/pounds) in the (dollar-franc/dollar-pound) market, spending all your $100,000. This gets you _____ in (pounds/francs).

c. You place another order to sell everything you just acquired in (b) to obtain (francs/pounds/dollars) in the (franc-pound/dollar-franc/dollar-pound) market. This gets you _____ in (pounds/dollars/francs).

d. You place your last order to sell everything you just acquired in (c) to obtain (francs/pounds/dollars) in the (franc-pound/dollar-franc/dollar-pound) market. This gets you _____ in (pounds/dollars/francs).

e. Comparing the $100,000 you spent in (b) with what you just acquired in (d), you realize you just earned your firm _____ dollars of arbitrage profit in a few seconds. Not bad. Of course, as you watch the data on your screen start to change, it is clear other people have now caught on to the situation, too. As many other traders start placing orders just like yours, you expect to see that the price of the franc in the dollar-franc market (rise/fall), while the price of the pound in the franc-pound market will (rise/fall), and the price of the pound in the pound-dollar market will (rise/fall).

4. Suppose once again that the United States and France are the only two countries that trade with one another. Given current economic conditions in each country, American demand for French francs is again given by

$$D^{FF} = 14 - 40e,$$

but French supply of francs is

$$S^{FF} = 1.75 + 30e.$$

As before, D^{FF} is quantity of francs demanded, S^{FF} is quantity of francs supplied, both in hundreds of millions per day. The variable e in both equations is the exchange rate, giving the dollar price of a unit of French currency.

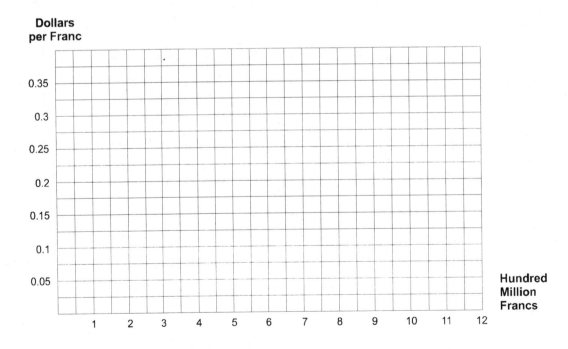

a. Solve the demand and supply equations to determine the equilibrium exchange rate and quantity of francs traded. The equilibrium exchange rate is _____ dollars per franc. Plot these demand and supply curves for French francs. Label them D^{FF}_1 and S^{FF}_1.

b. Suppose that equilibrium real GDP in the United States is above its full-employment level. American policy-makers have considered their options, and decided to use monetary policy to bring equilibrium real GDP to its full-employment level. To do that, the Fed will have to (increase/decrease) the money supply. This will (increase/decrease) the interest rate and so (increase/decrease) interest-sensitive spending. Equilibrium real GDP will then (increase/decrease) to its full-employment level through the usual multiplier process. If, in a closed economy, the money supply would have to change by $50 billion to achieve this policy goal. In an open economy we know that the required change in the money supply will be (greater/smaller) than $50 billion. Because of its impact on the exchange rate, monetary policy is (less/more) effective in a an open economy than it is in a closed economy.

c. If the Fed pursues the policy described in (b), there will be an impact on the foreign exchange market. The U.S. interest rate will (fall/rise), and this will make French assets (more/less) attractive to American buyers compared to American assets. As American buyers (increase/decrease) their purchases of French assets, the (demand for/supply of) French francs will shift (leftward/rightward). This effect, alone, will tend to make the franc (appreciate/depreciate) and to make the dollar (appreciate/depreciate). Suppose the amount of this shift is FF 1.5 hundred million at every exchange rate. Plot the resulting demand or supply curve and label it appropriately.

d. In addition, as the Fed pursues the policy described in (b) and the U.S. interest rate (falls/rises) as described in (c), this will make American assets (more/less) attractive to French buyers compared to French assets. As French buyers (increase/decrease) their purchases of American assets, the (demand for/supply of) French francs will shift (leftward/rightward). This effect, alone, will tend to make the franc (appreciate/depreciate) and to make the dollar (appreciate/depreciate). Suppose the amount of this shift is FF 2 hundred million at every exchange rate. Plot the resulting demand or supply curve and label it appropriately.

e. Together, the effects described in (c) and (d) cause the franc to (appreciate/depreciate) and the dollar to (appreciate/depreciate). From the graph, we can see that, in the end, the exchange rate (increased/decreased) from _____ dollars per franc in part (a) to _____ dollars per franc in part (d).

15-MINUTE PRACTICE TEST

Set a timer, giving yourself just 15 minutes to answer all of the following questions. To see what you *really* know and remember, take the test at least a day *after* you've read the chapter in the text and completed the exercises in this study guide.

Multiple Choice: Circle the letter in front of the single best answer.

1. In the yen-dollar market, which of the following would shift the demand curve for Japanese yen rightward?
   a. An increase in real GDP in Japan
   b. An increase in the U.S. interest rate
   c. An increase in the Japanese price level
   d. All of the above
   e. None of the above

2. In the yen-dollar market, which of the following would shift the supply curve for Japanese yen rightward?
   a. An increase in real GDP in Japan
   b. An increase in the Japanese price level
   c. An increase in the U.S. interest rate
   d. All of the above
   e. None of the above

3. In the very short run (e.g., day to day), the most important influence on exchange rates is changes in
   a. relative inflation rates.
   b. the business cycle.
   c. relative interest rates.
   d. purchasing power parity.
   e. tastes for foreign goods.

4. Bilateral arbitrage assures us that
   a. similar goods will cost the same in different countries.
   b. inflation rates will tend to be similar among countries that trade with each other.
   c. a rise in a country's interest rate will cause its currency to appreciate.
   d. the exchange rate between any two currencies will be the same regardless of the country in which foreign currency is bought.
   e. the price of foreign currency will be the same whether the foreign currency is purchased directly or indirectly (i.e., through a third currency).

5. "You should go to Portugal, man. Everything there is, like, dirt cheap." If this statement is true, it is an apparent violation of

   a. comparative advantage.
   b. bilateral arbitrage.
   c. triangular arbitrage.
   d. the law of demand.
   e. purchasing power parity.

6. Under a managed float, a government will

   a. never intervene in the foreign exchange market.
   b. occasionally intervene in the foreign exchange market.
   c. fix the exchange rate against the currency of its trading partner.
   d. restrict the flow of capital into and out of the country.
   e. set up two different exchange rates: one for exports and another for imports.

7. If a country fixes its exchange rate below the equilibrium value, so its currency is artificially cheap to foreigners, it must

   a. buy its own currency in the foreign exchange market.
   b. sell its own currency in the foreign exchange market.
   c. sell other countries' currencies in the foreign exchange market.
   d. get permission from the United States and other powerful economies.
   e. raise its interest rates higher than they would be under a floating rate.

8. With floating exchange rates, an increase in government purchases causes GDP to rise by less when we take foreign trade into account, because the rise in G causes a

   a. fall in the interest rate.
   b. depreciation of the domestic currency.
   c. rise in net exports.
   d. all of the above.
   e. none of the above.

9. According to what you have learned in the chapter, which of the following would worsen a foreign currency crisis?

   a. The country in crisis raises its interest rate.
   b. The country in crisis discovers and announces previously unknown reserves of foreign currency.
   c. Residents of the country in crisis develop an increased taste for foreign goods.
   d. Residents of other countries develop an increased taste for the goods of the country in crisis.
   e. All of the above.

10. Under floating exchange rates, which of the following would cause U.S. net exports to decrease?

    a. A decrease in the U.S. money supply.
    b. An appreciation of the dollar.
    c. A depreciation of the currency of one of our major trading partners/
    d. All of the above
    e. None of the above

True/False: For each of the following statements, circle T if the statement is true or F if the statement is false.

T   F   1. "Hot money" explains how exchange rates are determined in the long run.

T   F   2.   If exchange rates float, an increase in the U.S. interest rate will cause the U.S. dollar to appreciate against the currencies of its trading partners.

T   F   3. An increase in U.S. GDP will cause the supply curve for British pounds to shift rightward.

T   F   4. Bilateral arbitrage works to make the exchange rate between any two currencies the same, no matter in which country the currency is purchased.

T   F   5. Under a managed float, a country's central bank sometimes buys its own currency to prevent it from depreciating, and sells its own currency to prevent it from appreciating.

T   F   6. With floating exchange rates, an increase in the U.S. money supply will cause the U.S. dollar to depreciate and net exports to increase.

T   F   7. If a country fixes its currency against the dollar, and currently the fixed exchange rate is the same as the equilibrium exchange rate, then a sudden decrease in that country's interest rate would require it to begin buying its own currency in the foreign exchange market.

T   F   8. If a country has a trade deficit, it must also have a net capital inflow.

ANSWERS TO QUESTIONS

ANSWERS FOR CHAPTER 1

Speaking Economics

1. economics
2. scarcity
3. resources
4. labor
5. capital
6. human capital
7. land
8. microeconomics
9. macroeconomics
10. positive economics
11. normative economics
12. model
13. simplifying assumption
14. critical assumption

Chapter Highlights

1. scarcity
2. resources
3. land; labor; capital
4. micro
5. macro
6. positive
7. normative
8. abstract
9. conclusions
10. critical

Important Concepts

1. a. microeconomic; positive
   b. macroeconomic; positive
   c. microeconomic; positive
   d. microeconomic; normative
   e. macroeconomic; positive
   f. microeconomic; normative
   g. macroeconomic; normative

2. a. labor
   b. capital
   c. capital
   d. land
   e. labor
   f. capital
   g. labor
   h. capital

3. False: The right amount of detail depends on the purpose for which the model will be used. In general, a model should have as few details as possible to accomplish its purpose.

4. False: The two types are "simplifying assumptions" and "critical assumptions."

Skills and Tools

1. a.

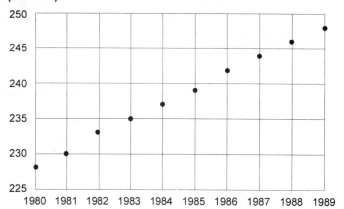

b. (iv)

c.

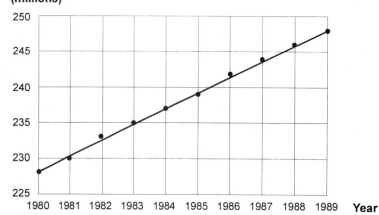

d. Population increased by approximately 2.24 million per year. Your answer can differ from this by a bit because it will depend on how you drew your line with the ruler. To get your answer, though, calculate how much population increased along the vertical axis (the rise) as you move from any one year to the next year along the horizontal axis (the run) on the line you drew.

2. a. 30 to 60; 90 to 120; positive
   b. 0 to 30; 60 to 90; negative
   c. Maximum value of $Y = 1,000$ is achieved at $X = 60$; Minimum value of $Y = 200$ is achieved at $X = 90$.

3.

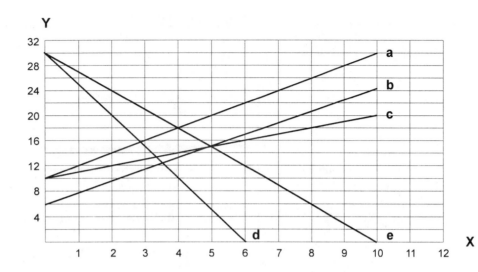

a. 10; 2; increases; constant
b. 5; 2; increases; constant
c. 10; 1; increases; constant
d. 30; −5; decreases; constant
e. 30; −3; decreases; constant

10-Minute Practice Test

Multiple Choice

1. c
2. e
3. d
4. b

4. b
5. c
6. b

True/False

1. F
2. F
3. F

4. T
5. F

ANSWERS FOR CHAPTER 2

Speaking Economics

1. opportunity cost
2. production possibilities frontier (PPF)
3. law of increasing opportunity cost.
4. productive inefficiency
5. specialization
6. exchange
7. absolute advantage
8. comparative advantage
9. resource allocation
10. traditional economy
11. command economy; centrally planned economy
12. market economy
13. market

14. price
15. communism
16. socialism

17. capitalism
18. economic system

Chapter Highlights

1. opportunity cost
2. opportunity cost; resources
3. increasing; greater
4. inefficient
5. specialization; exchange; specialization; exchange

6. absolute advantage
7. comparative advantage
8. comparative advantage
9. command
10. market

Important Concepts

1. False; if the individual had not gone to college, he/she would only have had *one* of the full-time jobs, not all three of them. To determine the foregone income, we would use the job that *would* have been chosen if the person did not go to college. If, for example, the person would have chosen to be a truck driver, then the opportunity cost of a year in college would be the direct money cost of college plus $45,000 in foregone income.

2. The law of increasing opportunity cost.

3. In any order
   (a) productive inefficiency
   (b) recession.

4. In any order
   (a) The development of expertise from specializing in a single task
   (b) the reduction in unproductive time to switch among different tasks
   (c) gains from comparative advantage.

5. Yes, this is consistent with comparative advantage. College professors have a comparative advantage in other activities, such as writing research papers and teaching. The opportunity cost of locating library materials is higher for them than for their students.

6. In any order
   (a) tradition
   (b) command
   (c) the market

7. In any order
   (a) communism
   (b) socialism
   (c) capitalism

8. In any order
   a. market capitalism – resource allocation by the market; private resource ownership
   b. centrally planned capitalism – resource allocation by command; private resource ownership
   c. centrally planned socialism – resource allocation by command; state resource ownership
   d. market socialism – resource allocation by the market; state resource ownership

Skills and Tools

1. a.

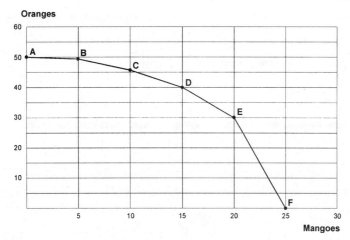

   b. 1; 5; 5; 1
      5; 3; 3
      5; 6; 5; 10; 5; 30;   increasing

   c. 5; 30; 30; 5
      10; 5; 5
      6; 5; 3; 5;   increasing

2. a. are not; zero; zero; no
   b. cannot; improve; acquire more

3. Constant; 50; Y; 50; Y; 50; Y; constant

4. Increases; less than; greater than

5. a. sweaters; fish
   b. 2; 1/3; fish; sweaters

15-Minute Practice Test

Multiple Choice

1. c	6. e
2. d	7. d
3. a	8. c
4. b	9. a
5. b	10. e

True/False
1. F
2. F
3. T
4. T

5. F
6. T
7. F
8. F

ANSWERS FOR CHAPTER 3

Speaking Economics

1. aggregation
2. imperfectly competitive market
3. perfectly competitive market
4. individual's quantity demanded
5. market quantity demanded
6. law of demand
7. demand schedule
8. demand curve
9. change in quantity demanded
10. change in demand
11. income
12. wealth
13. normal good
14. inferior good

15. substitute
16. complement
17. technology
18. firm's quantity supplied
19. market quantity supplied
20. law of supply
21. supply schedule
22. supply curve
23. change in quantity supplied
24. change in supply
25. alternate good
26. equilibrium
27. excess demand
28. excess supply

Chapter Highlights

1. market
2. buyers, sellers (either order)
3. imperfectly competitive
4. competitive (or perfectly competitive); price (or market price)
5. competitive (or perfectly competitive)
6. demanded; price
7. market quantity demanded; price
8. law; fall
9. demand curve; price
10. downward
11. quantity demanded
12. shift; change in demand
13. income, wealth (either order); income, wealth (either order); right
14. increase; right
15. decrease; left
16. technology; inputs; outputs
17. prices; price
18. supplied; price

19. market quantity supplied
20. increase
21. price; price
22. upward
23. quantity supplied
24. shift; change in supply
25. decrease; left
26. rises; falls; left
27. increase; right
28. right
29. decrease; left
30. equilibrium
31. equilibrium; equilibrium
32. left
33. right
34. market; market; market
35. goals; constraints; goals; constraints
36. equilibrium; equilibrium; equilibrium
37. equilibrium

Important Concepts

1. Income (decrease, since it's a normal good); wealth (decrease, since it's a normal good); price of a substitute (decrease); price of a complement (increase); population (decrease); expectations (e.g., an expectation that the price will *fall* in the future); tastes (a change in tastes *away* from the good).

2. Prices of inputs (decrease); profitability of alternate good (decrease); technology (e.g., a cost-saving technological advance); productive capacity (increase, e.g. from an increase in the number of firms); expected future price of the good (decrease).

3. In a perfectly competitive market, there are so many small buyers and sellers that *no one of them can influence the market price*. Each buyer and seller takes the market price as given. In an imperfectly competitive market, at least some buyers or sellers have the ability to influence the price of the product.

4. False. Income is what you earn over a *period* of time. Your wealth is the total value of what you own, minus what you owe, at a given *moment* in time.

5. False. A "change in demand" refers only to a shift in the demand curve. The phrase, "change in quantity demanded" is used for a movement along the demand curve.

Skills and Tools

1. a.

   b. 10; fall; 2; rise; 18

2. a.

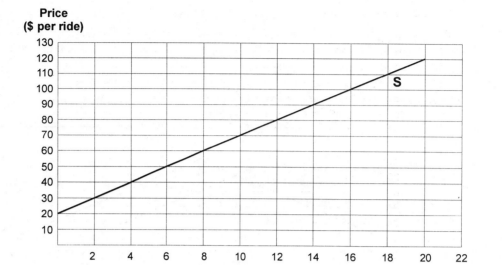

b.   6; rise; 14; fall; 2

3.

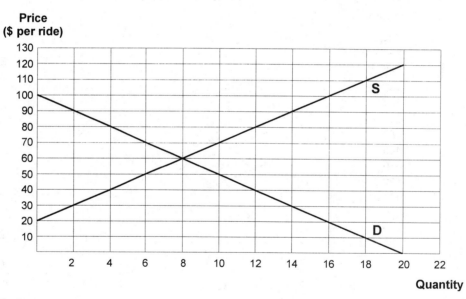

a.   60; 8
b.   supply; 8; fall sellers; sell
c.   demand; 8; rise; buyers; buy

4. a. $120
    b. increase; rightward
    c.
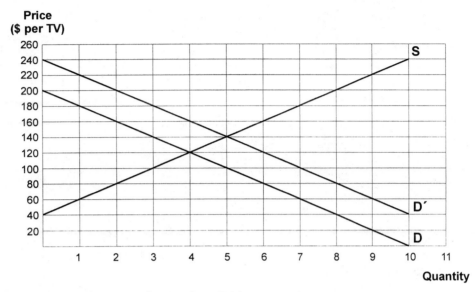

    d. Equilibrium price is now $140, where D´ intersects S
    e. decrease; leftward
    f.
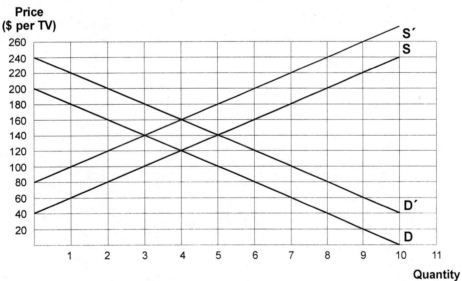

    g. Equilibrium price is now $160, where S´ intersects D´

5. a.

P	Q^D	Q^S
$450	20	80
400	30	70
350	40	60
300	50	50
250	60	40
200	70	30
150	80	20^3

b. supplied; demanded; excess supply; 40; fall; $300
c. demanded; supplied; excess demand; 60; rise; $300

6.

P	Q^D	Q^S
$270	2	20
210	6	15
90	14	5
30	18	0

ANSWERS FOR CHAPTER 4

Speaking Economics

1. business cycles
2. expansion
3. peak
4. recession

5. trough
6. depression
7. aggregation

Chapter Highlights

1. stable prices (or low inflation)
2. real gross domestic product (or real GDP)

3. unemployment rate
4. expansion; peak; recession; trough
5. aggregation

Important Concepts

1. (in any order): rapid economic growth, high employment; stable prices (or low inflation)

2. An expansion is a period of rising output; a peak occurs when output reaches its highest point during an expansion.

3. Disagreement can be positive (about how the economy works) or normative (about what we should do about the economy, based on our differing values).

10-Minute Practice Test

Multiple Choice
1. e
2. d
3. b
4. c

5. d
6. c
7. b
8. c

True/False
1. F   4. F
2. F   5. F
3. T

ANSWERS FOR CHAPTER 5

Speaking Economics

1. gross domestic product (GDP)   16. factor payments
2. intermediate good   17. factor payments approach
3. final good   18. nominal variable
4. flow variable   19. real variable
5. stock variable   20. nonmarket production
6. expenditure approach   21. frictional unemployment
7. consumption   22. seasonal unemployment
8. capital stock   23. structural unemployment
9. private investment   24. cyclical unemployment
10. net investment   25. full employment
11. government purchases   26. potential output
12. transfer payments   27. labor force
13. net exports   28. unemployment rate
14. value added   29. involuntary part-time workers
15. value added approach   30. discouraged workers

Chapter Highlights

1. gross domestic product; final; the   10. intermediate goods
   nation's borders   11. firms
2. intermediate; final; intermediate; final   12. factor
3. flow   13. firms; profit; households
4. expenditure   14. income (or factor payments)
5. households   15. nominal; real
6. plant, equipment (either order): home;   16. nominal; current; purchasing
   inventories (or inventory stocks)   17. Short; short
7. (either order): private; government   18. cyclical; (any order): seasonal, frictional,
8. Transfer; transfers (or transfer   structural
   payments); purchases   19. consume
9. net; imports

Important Concepts

1. GDP is the total value of all final goods and services produced for the marketplace during a
   given year, within the nation's borders.

2. (any order): expenditure approach; factor payments approach; value added approach

3. a. yes; G
   b. no; nothing produced
   c. no; nothing produced
   d. yes; C

   e. no; nothing produced
   f. yes; I
   g. yes; NX
   h. yes; I

4. a. flow
   b. flow
   c. stock
   d. stock

   e. stock
   f. flow
   g. flow
   h. flow

5. (any order): seasonal; frictional; structural; cyclical

Skills and Tools

1. a. $5,490
   b. $1,221
   c. $1,476
   d. $106
   e. $8,293
   f. Wear and tear on factory equipment, Existing homes which were destroyed, Depreciation of government assets, Transfer payments

2. a. (See table.)

	Firm	Cost of Intermediate Goods	Revenue	Value Added
Cars	Rubber Company	$0.00	$0.75	$0.75
	Tire Company	$0.75	$1.50	$0.75
	Steel Company	$0.00	$2.00	$2.00
	Car Manufacturer	$3.50	$4.00	$0.50
	Car Dealer	$4.00	$4.50	$0.50
Food	Farmer	$0.00	$0.75	$0.75
	Supermarket	$0.75	$1.00	$0.25

   b. $5.50

3. a. $930
   b. $315
   c. $150
   d. $1,605
   e. $3,000
   f. $350 of the total revenue of Summertime Farming comes from the sale of intermediate goods to Savory Sandwiches. This $350 is not included when calculating GDP using the expenditure approach, because it is already included in spending on the final goods produced by Savory Farms. Other than the this $350, the rest of the total revenue

represents sales of final goods, so GDP is $1,400 - $350 + $1,950 = $3,000, just as we found using the factor payments approach in e. above.

4. a. 212 million; 148.5 million; 4.7%
   b. remain unchanged; 148.5 million
   c. remain unchanged; remain unchanged
   d. decrease; decrease; 3.4%
   e. decrease; decrease; 2.7%
   f. decrease; 0%
   g. increase; increase; 6.0%

15-Minute Practice Test

Multiple Choice

1. d   6. e
2. d   7. e
3. b   8. a
4. c   9. d
5. b   10. e

True/False

1. F   5. F
2. F   6. T
3. T   7. F
4. T   8. F

ANSWERS FOR CHAPTER 6

Speaking Economics

1. unit of value   9. deflation
2. means of payment   10. indexation
3. Federal Reserve System   11. nominal variable
4. fiat money   12. real variable
5. price level   13. GDP price index
6. index   14. nominal interest rate
7. Consumer Price Index (CPI) 15. real interest rate
8. inflation rate

Chapter Highlights

1. nominal; nominal; 100   8. resources
2. GDP; consumer   9. more rapidly; more slowly; over-
3. average   10. over
4. purchasing power   11. over
5. the rate of inflation   12. over
6. anticipated (or expected) 13. increase
7. inaccurate; higher; lower

Important Concepts

1. Commodity money has some value in itself, because it has an important non-money use. Fiat money has no intrinsic value; it is money because the government declares that it is money.

2. (either order): redistributive cost; resource cost.

3. (three of the following four, in any order): substitution bias—leads to *over*estimate; new technologies—leads to *over*estimate; quality changes—leads to *over*estimate; growth in discounting—leads to *over*estimate.

Skills and Tools

1. a. (See table.)

	Average Temperature (Degrees F)	**Temperature Index (May = 100)**
January	33	47.1
February	30	42.9
March	42	60.0
April	56	80.0
May	70	100.0
June	78	111.4
July	84	120.0
August	88	125.7
September	79	112.9
October	75	107.1
November	63	90.0
December	45	64.3

   b. increased; 100; 111.4; 11.4%; higher
   c. 90.0; 10%; lower
   d. February; October; April

2. a. (See graph.)

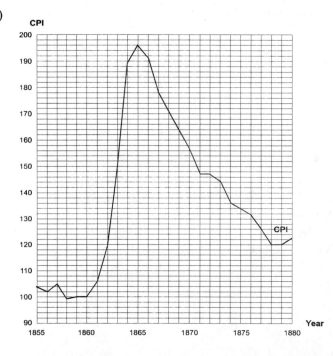

b. increased; 100; 196; 96%; higher; decreased; 23%; higher

c. (See table.)

Year	CPI	Inflation Rate	Year	CPI	Inflation Rate
1860	100		1865	196	
		6.0%			−2.6%
1861	106		1866	191	
		14.2%			−6.8%
1862	121		1867	178	
		24.8%			−3.9%
1863	151		1868	171	
		25.2 %			−4.1%
1864	189		1869	164	
		3.7%			−4.3%
1865	196		1870	157	

d. inflation; inflation; 3.7%; 1864; 1865; 25.2%; 1863; 1864

e. deflation; deflation; 1866; 1867

3. a. increased every year; increased every year

   b. (See graph.)

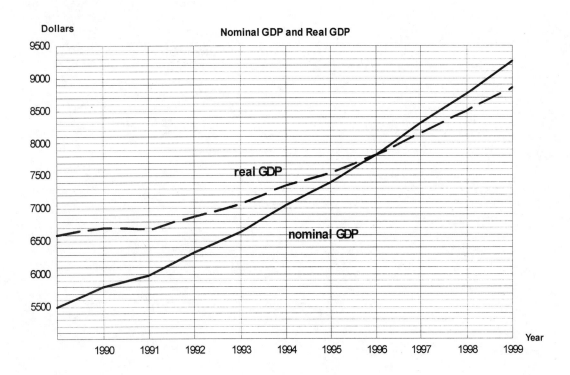

c. did not; decreased; 6,136.3; 6,079.4; increased; 5,743.8; 5,916.7; increased; 93.6; 97.3; decreased; increased; increased; greater; increased

4. a. (See table.)

Year	Prime Bank Interest Rate (Nominal)	Inflation Rate	Prime Bank Interest (Real)
1989	10.9%	4.2%	6.7%
1990	10.0%	4.3%	5.7%
1991	8.5%	4.0%	4.5%
1992	6.3%	2.8%	3.5%
1993	6.0%	2.6%	3.4%
1994	7.1%	2.4%	4.7%
1995	8.8%	2.6%	6.2%
1996	8.3%	2.2%	6.1%
1997	8.4%	2.0%	6.4%
1998	8.4%	1.0%	7.4%
1999	8.0%	1.5%	6.5%

b. (See graph.)

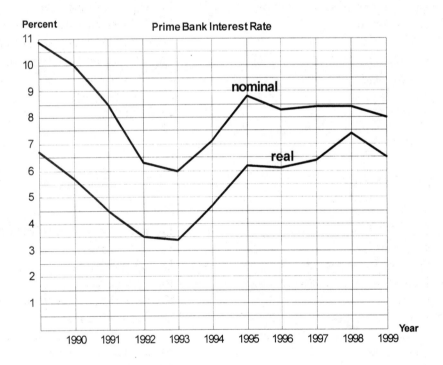

15-Minute Practice Test

Multiple Choice

1. b
2. e
3. c
4. b
5. d

6. d
7. a
8. d
9. c
10. b

True/False

1.	F	5.	T
2.	F	6.	T
3.	F	7.	F
4.	T	8.	F

ANSWERS FOR CHAPTER 7

Speaking Economics

1. classical model
2. market clearing
3. labor supply curve
4. labor demand curve
5. aggregate production function
6. circular flow
7. Say's law
8. net taxes
9. (household) saving
10. leakages
11. injections
12. planned investment spending
13. loanable funds market
14. budget deficit
15. budget surplus
16. national debt
17. supply of funds curve
18. investment demand curve
19. government demand for funds curve
20. total demand for funds curve
21. fiscal policy
22. crowding out
23. complete crowding out

Chapter Highlights

1. classical
2. markets clear
3. resources
4. upward; increases; rise
5. increases; rise; downward
6. classical
7. labor; technology
8. potential (or full-employment)
9. output
10. Say
11. injections; net taxes; government purchases
12. deficit; G – T; surplus; T - G
13. State; local; deficit; deficit; surplus; surplus
14. interest rate
15. falls; downward
16. interest rate
17. rises; remains unchanged; rises
18. loanable funds
19. government; net taxes; output
20. decrease; increase
21. classical; private
22. loanable funds; businesses

Important Concepts

1. Markets clear. This means that the price adjusts in every market until quantity supplied and quantity demanded are equal.

2. The labor market; the aggregate production function

3. The loanable funds market

4. Leakages (either order): saving; net taxes. Injections (either order): investment spending; government purchases.

5. a. no change   d. increase
   b. no change   e. decrease
   c. increase

Skills and Tools

1. a. (See graph.)

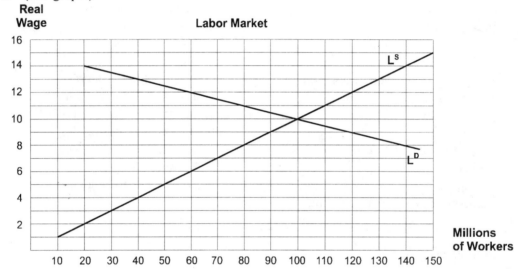

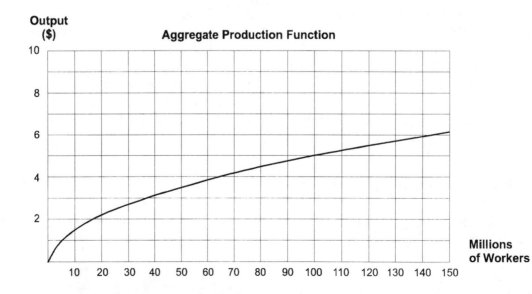

b. 60; 120; excess supply; fall below
c. 140; 80; excess demand; rise above
d. 100; 100; equilibrium; remain at
e. (See the graph.)
f. $5 trillion

2. a. (See graph.)

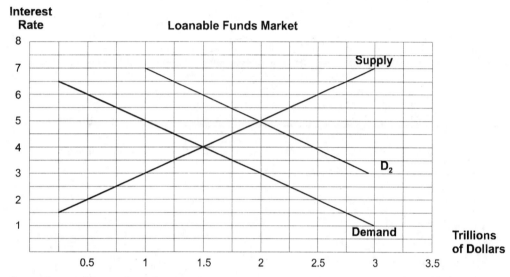

b. rises; demand; negative; decreases
c. deficit; .5, G – T = .5; deficit; demand; borrow; .5
d. add; Total Demand = 3.0 – (1/2)*r* + .5 = 3.5 – (1/2)*r* (See graph.)
e. excess supply; fall below; excess demand rise above; 4%
f. 1.5; deficit; .5; 1.0; 1.5; 1.5

g.

Flows in the Economy of Upper Classica
(Trillions of Dollars)

Total Output		5.0
Total Income		5.0
Consumption Spending (C)		2.5
Investment Spending (I)		1.0
Government Spending (G)		1.5
Net Tax Revenue (T)	1.0	
Household Saving (S)	1.5	

h. equal; S + T; 2.5; I + G; 2.5; does

3. a. demand curve; rightward; $1; demand (See following graph.)
   b. rise, 5; increase; increase; decrease; increase
   c. increase; increase; 0.5; decrease; 0.5; decreases; 0.5; decrease; the same amount; did

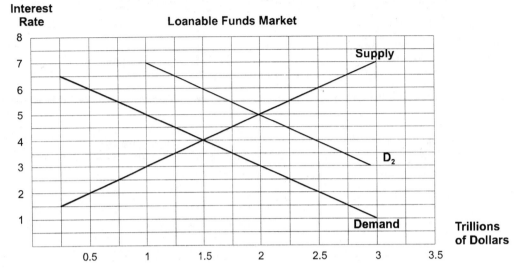

15-Practice Test

Multiple Choice

1. a	6. b
2. e	7. b
3. b	8. b
4. c	9. b
5. a	10. e

True/False

1. F	5. T
2. F	6. T
3. F	7. F
4. T	8. T

ANSWERS FOR CHAPTER 8

Speaking Economics

1. average standard of living
2. productivity (or labor productivity)
3. capital per worker
4. corporate profits tax
5. investment tax credit
6. capital gains tax
7. consumption tax
8. human capital
9. technological change
10. patent protection

Chapter Highlights

1. long; short
2. the population; rise; the population; fall
3. rightward; rightward
4. supply
5. demand
6. decrease; decrease
7. employment; employment
8. taxes; rightward
9. saving
10. growing; reduce; increase
11. investment
12. human; upward
13. human
14. R&D; R&D
15. tradeoffs
16. tradeoffs; costs
17. cuts
18. consumption (or consumer)
19. increase; increase
20. growth; growth
21. population
22. (either order): consumption, capital; consumption; capital

Important Concepts

1. a. labor market diagram; labor supply curve shifts rightward
   b. labor market diagram; labor supply curve shifts rightward
   c. labor market diagram; labor supply curve shifts rightward
   d. labor market diagram; labor demand curve shifts rightward
   e. loanable funds market diagram; investment demand curve, and therefore the total demand for funds curve, shifts rightward
   f. loanable funds market diagram; supply of funds curve (household saving) shifts rightward. (Note: as a result of the increase in investment, the capital stock will grow more rapidly, so the aggregate production function will shift up more rapidly as well.)
   g. loanable funds market diagram; budget deficit, and therefore the total demand for funds curve, shifts leftward. (Note: as a result of the drop in the interest rate, investment will increase, the capital stock will grow more rapidly, and the aggregate production function will shift up more rapidly as well.)
   h. loanable funds market diagram; the supply of funds curve, shifts rightward.
   i. aggregate production function diagram; aggregate production function shifts upward

2. (three of the following four, in any order): budgetary costs; consumption costs; opportunity costs of workers' time; sacrifice of other social goals

3. (in any order): very low output per capital; high population growth rates; poor infrastructure

Skills and Tools

1. a.; b.; and c (See graph.)

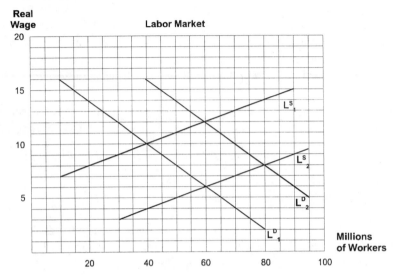

d. 10; 40; 16; (16/40 or 0.4)
e. right; (See graph labeled L^D_2.)
f. 12; 60; 21; (21/60 or 0.35); increased; increased; increased; decreased
g. right (See graph labeled L^S_2.)
h. 8; 80; 24; (24/80 or 0.3); decreased; increased; increased; decreased
i. decreased; $10; $8; increased; 40 million; 80 million; increased; $16 trillion; $24 trillion; decreased; (16/40 or 0.4); (24/80 or 0.3); decrease; decrease

2. a. $10; 40 million; $16 trillion; (16/40 or 0.4)
    b. (See following graph.)
    c. be unaffected; be unaffected; rise; rise; $10; 40 million; $20 trillion dollars; (20/40 or 0.5)
    d. increase; decrease; increase; increase; decrease
    e. 0.40; $12; 60 million; $6; 60 million; (24/60 or 0.4)

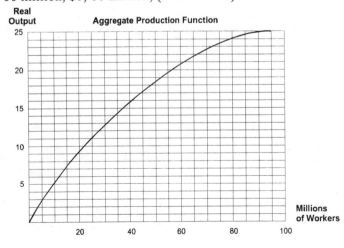

15-Minute Practice Test

Multiple Choice

1. b
2. c
3. b
4. d
5. d

6. b
7. c
8. d
9. e
10. a

True/False

1. F
2. T
3. F
4. F

5. T
6. F
7. F
8. F

ANSWERS FOR CHAPTER 9

Speaking Economics

1. boom
2. disequilibrium

3. spending shock

Chapter Highlights

1. (either order): labor demand, labor supply; (either order): labor demand, labor supply
2. short; clears; clears; short
3. opportunity cost
4. wage rate
5. equlibrium

6. greater
7. increase; greater;
8. decrease; less;
9. above;
10. normal
11. below;
12. normal

Important Concepts

1. (either order): Sudden shifts in labor supply are unlikely to occur; even if they occurred, they could not accurately explain the facts of recessions, in which employment drops in spite of workers' desire to work.

2. In a recession, the benefit to the firm is greater than the opportunity cost to the worker. In a boom, the opportunity cost to the worker is greater than the benefit to the firm.

3. The difference between the opportunity cost to the worker and the benefit to the firm imply that mutual gains are possible by increasing or decreasing employment.

Skills and Tools

1. a. (See the following graph.) $12; 120
   b. disequilibrium; below; in a recession
   c. 8; 16; exceeds; are; increase; rise above
   d. decrease; increase; 120; 12; 12; 12; would not; equilibrium; long run equilibrium

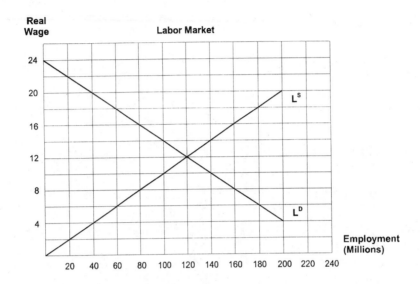

2. a. $12; 120
   b. disequilibrium; above; in a boom
   c. risen; 12; 16; 16; 8; is exceeded by; let some workers go; decrease; fall below
   d. 120; 12; 12; 12; equilibrium; long run equilibrium

10-Minute Practice Test

Multiple Choice

1. c	4. b
2. e	5. b
3. a	6. c

True/False

1. T	4. T
2. F	5. T
3. F	

ANSWERS FOR CHAPTER 10

Speaking Economics

1. short-run macro model
2. disposable income
3. consumption function
4. autonomous consumption
5. marginal propensity to consume (MPC)
6. consumption-income line
7. aggregate expenditure (AE)
8. equilibrium GDP
9. expenditure multiplier
10. automatic stabilizers

Chapter Highlights

1. (either order): consumption, income; (either order): income, consumption; (either order): consumption, income
2. consumption; disposable; disposable
3. zero; one
4. marginal propensity to consume (or MPC); marginal propensity to consume (or MPC)
5. income; anything else besides income
6. plant; new home; Inventory
7. investment; government; outside of
8. businesses; foreign; final; C +I^p+G+NX
9. MPC
10. fall; equilibrium
11. rise; equilibrium
12. (either order): output or GDP, agg. exp.
13. GDP or output; aggregate expenditure
14. 45-degree
15. 45-degree; inventories; reduce
16. 45-degree; inventories; increase
17. Equilibrium; 45-degree
18. spending; spending
19. spending; spending
20. equilibrium GDP
21. 1/(1 − MPC)
22. rise; fall
23. multiplier; multiplier
24. autonomous; net exports; aggregate expenditure; expenditure
25. stabilizer; reduces; more
26. zero; full-employment; zero
27. recession; bel0ow

Important Concepts

1. (any order)
   consumption spending (C)
   investment spending (I)
   government purchases (G)
   net exports (NX)

2. a.   C = a + bDI, where b is the MPC
   b.   1/(1 − MPC)
   c.   −MPC/(1 − MPC)

3. (any order)
   a decrease in autonomous consumption (a)
   a decrease in investment spending (I)
   a decrease in government purchases (G)
   a decrease in net exports (NX)
   an increase in net taxes (T).

4. Yes, equilibrium GDP would increase, but by exactly $100 billion. With an MPC of zero, the expenditure multiplier has a value of $1/(1 - 0) = 1$, so the $100 billion increase in G would be multiplied by 1 to get the rise in equilibrium GDP.

Skills and Tools

1. a. (See table.)

Income or GDP ($ Billions)	Tax Collections ($ Billions)	Disposable Income ($ Billions)	Consumption Spending ($ Billions)
3,000	1,000	2,000	2,500
3,500	1,000	2,500	2,750
4,000	1,000	3,000	3,000
4,500	1,000	3,500	3,250
5,000	1,000	4,000	3,500
5,500	1,000	4,500	3,750
6,000	1,000	5,000	4,000
6,500	1,000	5,500	4,250
7,000	1,000	6,000	4,500
7,500	1,000	6,500	4,750

b. (See graph.)

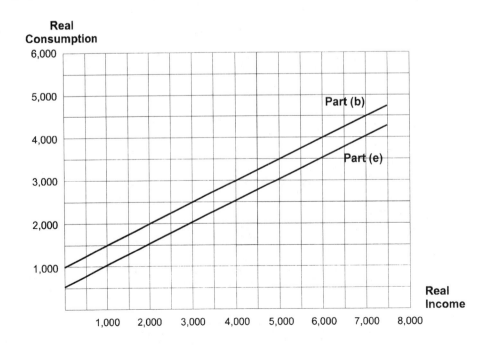

c. 0.5

d. decrease; $1,000; 0.5; decrease; $500; downward; $500

e. 0.5

f. decrease; increase; increase

2. a. (See table.)

Income or GDP ($ Billions)	Consumption Spending ($ Billions)	Investment Spending ($ Billions)	Government Purchases ($ Billions)	Aggregate Expenditure ($ Billions)
3,000	2,500	800	450	3,750
3,500	2,750	800	450	4,000
4,000	3,000	800	450	4,250
4,500	3,250	800	450	4,500
5,000	3,500	800	450	4,750
5,500	3,750	800	450	5,000
6,000	4,000	800	450	5,250
6,500	4,250	800	450	5,500
7,000	4,500	800	450	5,750
7,500	4,750	800	450	6,000

b. $C + I^p + G + NX$; rise; fall; equals

c. (See graph.)

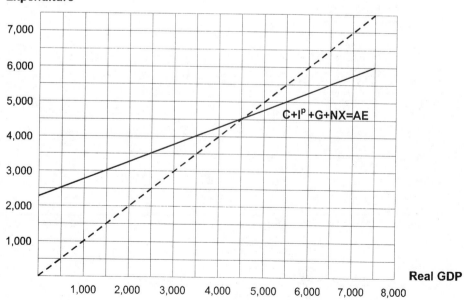

   d.   is not; $3,500; greater than; less output than; −1,000; increase their output; rise

   e.   is; $4,500; equal to; as much output as; 0; keep their output constant; remain constant

   f.   is not; $5,500; less than; more output than; 1,000; decrease their output; fall

   g.   below; too low; unemployment; increase; increase; rise to

3. a.   1/3

     b.   3/2 or 1.5

     c. $300 billion

     d.   decrease; $100 billion; decrease; $100 billion

     e.   downward; 100; (See graph.)

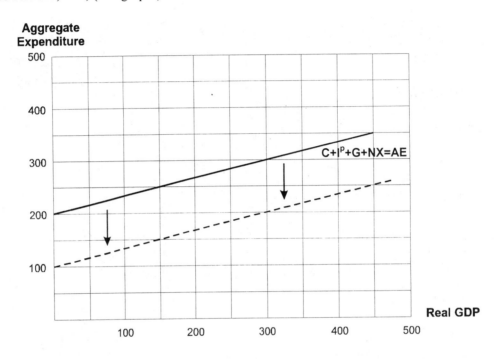

4. a.   (See table.)

Country	MPC	Multiplier	Change in Equilibrium GDP due to:			
			$\Delta I^P = +200$	$\Delta G = -100$	$\Delta a = +400$	$\Delta NX = -150$
1	0.40	1.67	333.33	-166.67	666.67	-250
2	0.50	2.00	400	−200	800	-300
3	0.60	2.50	500	−250	1,000	-375
4	0.75	4.00	800	-400	1,600	-600
5	0.80	5.00	1,000	−500	2,000	-750
6	0.90	10.00	2,000	−1,000	4,000	-1,500

     b.   increase; $100; 4; $400

     c.   decrease; $40; 5; $200

5. a. disposable income; subtracting; T; Y
    b. $C = 70 + 0.5Y$
    c. $AE = 200 + 0.5Y$
    d. $400 billion
    e. 0.5
    f. 2
    g. $430 billion

6. a. 0.5
    b. 2
    c. −1
    d. $10,000 billion
    e. decrease; 2,000; increase; 1,000

15-Minute Practice Test

Multiple Choice

1. b	6. c
2. d	7. e
3. e	8. e
4. d	9. c
5. e	10. d

True/False

1. T	5. F
2. F	6. T
3. T	7. T
4. F	8. T

ANSWERS FOR CHAPTER 11

Speaking Economics

1. liquidity
2. cash in the hands of the public
3. demand deposits
4. M1
5. M2
6. financial intermediary
7. balance sheet
8. bond
9. loan
10. reserves
11. required reserves
12. required reserve ratio
13. net worth
14. central bank
15. Federal Open Market Committee
16. discount rate
17. open market operations
18. excess reserves
19. demand deposit multiplier
20. run on the bank
21. banking panic

Chapter Highlights

1. cash; cash
2. cash; demand; checking account; travelers; cash; demand
3. owns; owes
4. reserves
5. government; open market operations
6. reserves
7. 1/RRR
8. required
9. secrecy
10. FDIC (or Federal Deposit Insurance Corporation)

Important Concepts

1. (any order): cash in the hands of the public; demand deposits; other checking account deposits; travelers checks

2. a. yes, assets
    b. yes, assets
    c. yes, assets
    d. no
    e. yes, liabilities
    f. yes, assets
    g. yes, liabilities

3. The FOMC includes all seven members of the board of governors, but it *also* includes five of the twelve Federal Reserve Bank Presidents on a rotating basis.

4. a. Nominates members of the Board of Governors, who serve on the FOMC
    b. Approves President's nominations for Board of Governors
    c. Help elect boards who select each of the 12 Federal Reserve Bank Presidents, who, in turn, rotate as members of the FOMC.

Skills and Tools

1. a. $1,103
    b. $2,948
    c. Public's credit limit on all credit cards; Public's stock market holdings

2. a. (See balance sheet.)

First Bank of Minnewaska

Assets		Liabilities and Net Worth	
Property and building	$21 million	Demand deposit	
Government bonds	$55 million	liabilities	$150 million
Loans to corporations	$20 million	Net worth	$21 million
Loans to private citizens	$45 million		
Cash in vault	$12 million		
In account with the Fed	$18 million		
Total Assets	$171 million	Total Liabilities plus Net Worth	$171 million

b. $21 million

c. $30 million; required; 0.2

3. a. increased; $5,000; excess reserves; 4,000; can make new loans; 4,000; increase; $4,000

   b. (See balance sheet.)

Changes in First Bank of Minnewaska's Balance Sheet

Action	Changes in Assets	Changes in Liabilities
Fed buys $5,000 bond from Sabre-Tooth Trading, which deposits $5,000 check from Fed deposits into its checking account:	+$5,000 in reserves	+$5,000 in demand deposits
First Bank lends out excess reserves in amount of $4,000 dollars:	−$4,000 in reserves +$4,000 in loans	
The total effect on First Bank from beginning to end:	+$1,000 in reserves +$4,000 in loans	+$5,000 in demand deposits

c. increased; 4,000; excess reserves; $3,200; can make new loans; $3,200; increase; $3,200

d. (See balance sheet.)

Changes in *Bank Too!'s* Balance Sheet

Action	Changes in Assets	Changes in Liabilities
Cindy deposits $4,000 Loan check into her checking account:	+$4,000 in reserves	+$4,000 in demand deposits
Bank Too! lends out excess reserves in amount of $3,200 dollars:	+$3,200 in reserves +$3,200 in loans	
The total effect on *Bank Too!* from beginning to end:	+$800 in reserves +$3,200 in loans	+$4,000 in demand deposits

e. (See table.)

Round	Change in Demand Deposits at This Bank	Change in Demand Deposits at All Banks
First Bank of Minnewaska	$5,000	$5,000
Bank Too!	$4,000	$9,000
Bank 3	$3,200	$12,200
Bank 4	$2,560	$14,760
Bank 5	$2,048	$16,808
Bank 6	$1,638	$18,446
Bank 7	$1,311	$19,757
Bank 8	$1,049	$20,806
…		
All Other Banks	$4,194	$25,000

f. makes new loans; creates; increase; 5

4. a. decreased; 2,000; deficient reserves; 1,600; must call in loans; $1,600; decrease; $1,600

b. (See balance sheet.)

Changes in First Bank of Minnewaska's Balance Sheet

Action	Changes in Assets	Changes in Liabilities
Fed sells $2,000 bond to SabreTooth, which pays with $2,000 check drawn on its checking account at First Bank.	−$2,000 in reserves	−$2,000 in demand deposits
First Bank calls in loans in amount of $1,600 dollars:	+$1,600 in reserves −$1,600 in loans	
The total effect on First Bank from beginning to end:	−$400 in reserves −$1,600 in loans	−$2,000 in demand deposits

c. (See table.)

Round	Change in Demand Deposits at This Bank	Change in Demand Deposits at All Banks
First Bank of Minnewaska	−$2,000	−$2,000
Bank 2	−$1,600	−$3,600
Bank 3	−$1,280	−$4,880
Bank 4	−$1,024	−$5,904
Bank 5	−$819	−$6,723
Bank 6	−$655	−$7,379
Bank 7	−$524	−$7,903
Bank 8	−$419	−$8,322
...		
All Other Banks	−$1,678	−$10,000

d. call in loans; extinguishes; decrease; 5

5. a. (See table on following page.)

Country	RRR	Demand Deposit Multiplier	Sale of $200	Purchase of $100	Sale of $400
1	0.1	10.0	−2,000	1,000	−4,000
2	0.2	5.0	−1,000	500	−2,000
3	0.4	2.5	−500	250	−1,000
4	0.5	2.0	−400	200	−800
5	0.8	1.25	−250	125	−500
6	1.0	1.0	−200	100	−400

Change in Money Supply due to Open Market:

b. increase; 1,000; purchases; decrease; decrease; buy; $200
c. decrease; 1,000; sales; increase; increase; sell; 500

15-Minute Practice Test

Multiple Choice

1. a
2. a
3. e
4. c
5. a
6. b
7. d
8. e
9. c
10. d

True/False

1. T
2. F
3. F
4. T
5. T
6. F
7. F
8. F

ANSWERS FOR CHAPTER 12

Speaking Economics

1. wealth constraint
2. money demand curve
3. money supply curve
4. excess supply of money
5. excess demand for bonds
6. federal funds rate

Chapter Highlights

1. wealth
2. interest
3. means of payment; interest; interest; means of payment
4. wealth; money
5. the interest rate; the interest rate
6. supply; right; supply; left
7. Equilibrium
8. demand
9. falls; rises
10. buying; falls; selling; rises
11. falls; durables; rises
12. upward; downward
13. interest rate
14. rise; investment
15. interest rate; interest rate
16. interest rate; interest rate
17. loanable funds; money
18. fall; rightward; rise

Important Concepts

1. money and bonds

2. a. money demand shifts leftward; b. money supply shifts leftward; c. money supply shifts rightward; d. money demand shifts rightward; e. money demand shifts leftward (because people expect the interest rate to fall and bond prices to rise); f. money demand shifts rightward (because income rises)

3. Monetary policy would be completely ineffective, since the channel through which it works—causing changes in the interest rate and then changes in consumption and investment spending—would be cut off.

4. a. decrease; b. increase; c. decrease; d. decrease; e. decrease (both because income goes down and because the interest rate rises); f. decreases (because the interest rate rises)

Skills and Tools

1. a. (See graph.)
   b. (See graph.)
   c. less than; excess supply; 250; excess demand; 250; buy more; rise; fall
   d. greater than; excess demand; 150; excess supply; $150; sell more; fall; rise
   e. 7; equal to; equilibrium; equal to

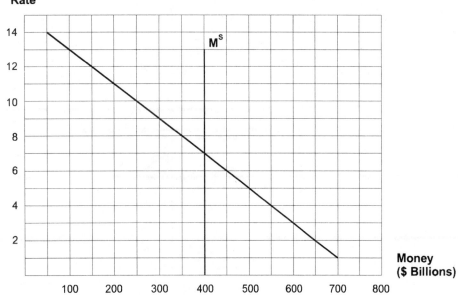

2. a. 8%
   b. increase; $200; 450; buy; 2; buy; $100
   c. (See graph.)
   d. decrease; $100; $150; sell; 2; sell; $50
   e. (See graph.)

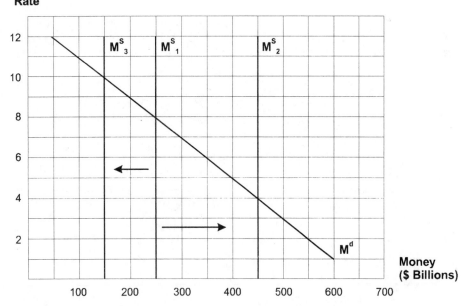

3. a. leftward; rise; 9; increase; decrease; consumption and planned investment; downward; decrease; a multiple of; decrease; demand; fall
   b. (See graph.)
   c. (See graph.)

Panel A

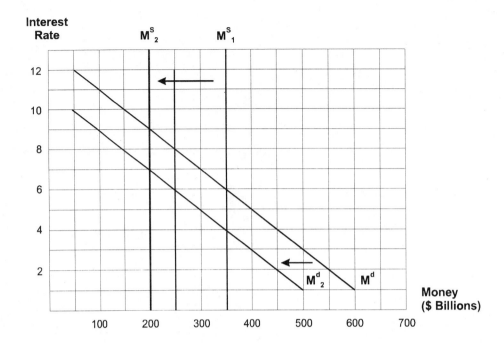

Panel B

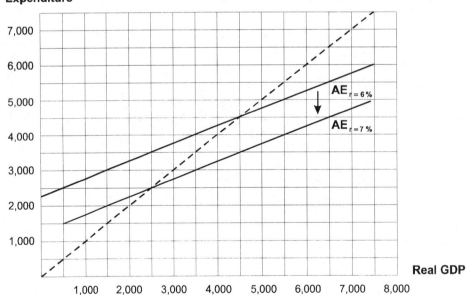

    d. fall; $25

 4. a. upward; $75; $150; $300; (See graph.)
     b. increase; demand; demand; rightward; rise; decrease; downward
     c. (See graph.)

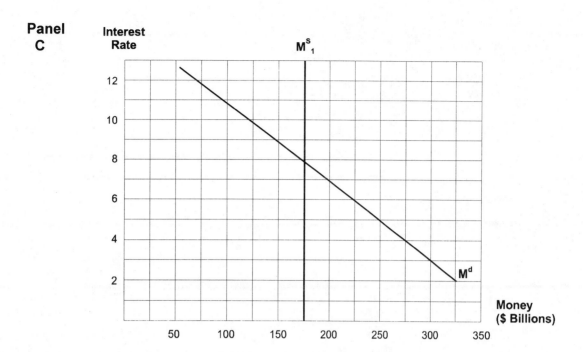

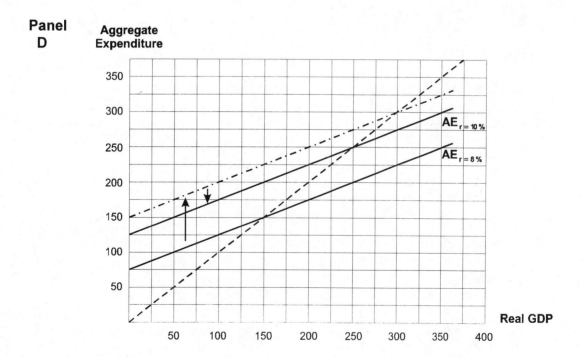

d. rise; crowded out; $25; $150; $300; $150; $250; will still cause GDP to rise but by a
    smaller multiple of any given change in spending

15-Minute Practice Test

Multiple Choice

1. c	6. d
2. b	7. b
3. e	8. d
4. d	9. a
5. d	10. e

True/False

1. F	5. T
2. F	6. T
3. F	7. F
4. T	8. F

ANSWERS FOR CHAPTER 13

Speaking Economics

1. aggregate demand (AD) curve
2. aggregate supply (AS) curve
3. short-run macroeconomic equilibrium
4. demand shock
5. supply shock
6. self-correcting mechanism
7. long-run aggregate supply curve
8. stagflation

Chapter Highlights

1. decrease; price level
2. the price level; the price level
3. investment; consumption; taxes
4. investment; consumption; taxes
5. increase; decrease
6. unit costs
7. markup; markup
8. rises; falls
9. wage
10. wage
11. rise; rise; fall; fall
12. price level; output
13. real GDP (or output); real GDP (or output)
14. demand shock; supply shock
15. AD; less; AD
16. rightward; rise; leftward; fall
17. rise; upward; fall; downward
18. full-employment (or potential)
19. self-correcting; rise; rise; decrease; fall; fall; increase
20. long
21. upward; increasing; downward; decreasing
22. supply

Important Concepts

1. a. increases
   b. decreases
   c. remains the same
   d. decreases
   e. decreases
   f. increases
   g. remains the same

2. a. increases
   b. increases
   c. remains the same
   d. increases
   e. increases
   f. remains the same

3. a. AD shifts rightward
   b. AD shifts leftward
   c. AD shifts rightward
   d. AD shifts rightward
   e. AS shifts upward
   f. AS shifts upward
   g. AS shifts downward

4.

	Event		
Short run effect on:	**the money supply decreases**	**government purchases decrease**	**world oil prices decrease**
the price level	decrease	decrease	decrease
output	decrease	decrease	increase
average nominal wage	no change	no change	no change

5.

	Event		
Long run effect on:	**the money supply decreases**	**government purchases decrease**	**world oil prices decrease**
the price level	decrease	decrease	no change
output	no change	no change	no change
average nominal wage	decrease	decrease	increase

Skills and Tools

1.

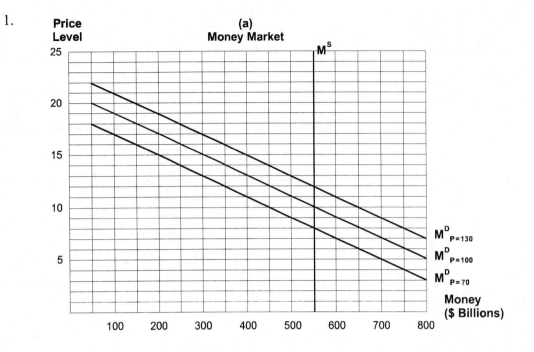

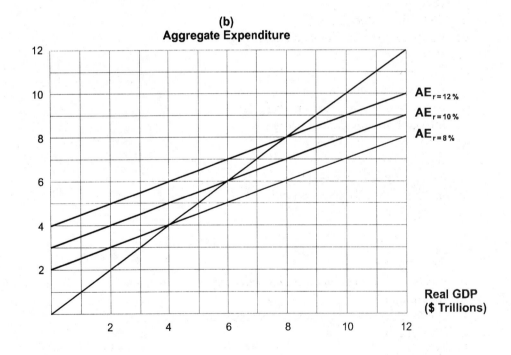

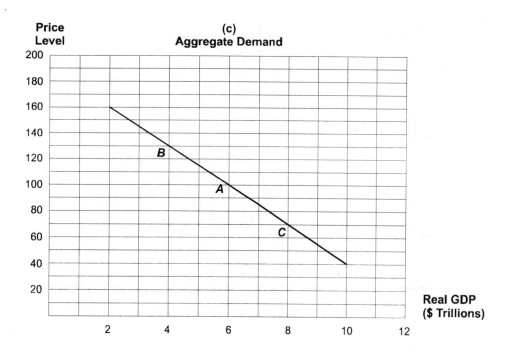

a. (See graph.); 10%.
b. (See graph.)
c. $6 trillion; (See graph.)
d. rightward; money demand curve
e. (See graph.); increase; 12
f. fall; downward
g. (See graph.); decrease; $4
h. decreases; $6; $4; (See graph.)
i. leftward; money demand curve
j. (See graph.); decrease; 8
k. rise; upward
l. (See graph.); increase; $8
m. increases; $6; $8; (See graph.)
n. (See graph.)

2. a. (See graph.)
   b. greater; increases; increase; increase; rise; raise; increase
   c. (See graph.)
   d. smaller; decreases; decrease; decrease; fall; lower; decrease
   e. (See graph.)
   f. (See graph.)

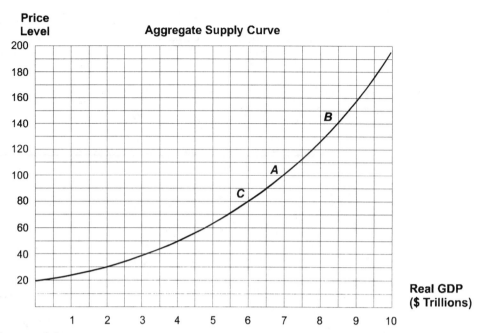

3. a. (See graph.)
   b. Yes; 100; $6 trillion
   c. increase; decrease; decrease; leftward
   d. (See graph.)
   e. decreases; decrease; decrease; decrease; fall; increase; decrease; less
   f. $4; 80
   g. below; high; down; downward; 60; $6 trillion
   h. (See graph.)

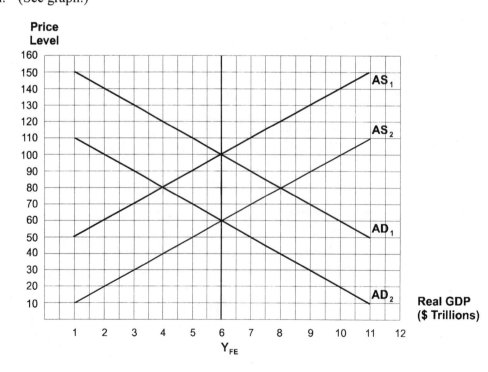

4. a. decrease; downward
   b. (See graph.); 90; $7 trillion
   c. above; low; up; upward; 100; $6 trillion
   d. (See graph.)

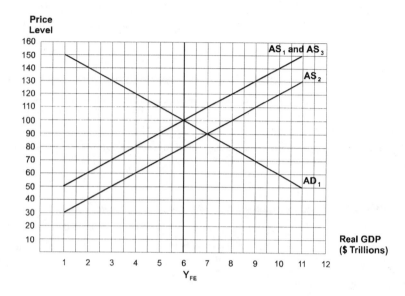

15-Minute Practice Test

Multiple Choice

1. d		6. b
2. d		7. b
3. d		8. d
4. a		9. e
5. c		10. d

True/False

1. F		5. F
2. T		6. F
3. T		7. F
4. T		8. T

ANSWERS FOR CHAPTER 14

Speaking Economics

1. natural rate of unemployment
2. passive monetary policy
3. active monetary policy
4. interest rate target
5. Phillips curve
6. long-run Phillips curve

Chapter Highlights

1. greater; smaller
2. money supply; price
3. price; increase; decrease
4. fall; rise
5. raise; fall; lower; rise
6. more (or higher) inflation; inflation
7. inflation; unemployment;
    unemployment; inflation
8. expectations
9. upward; upward
10. AD; recession
11. raise
12. inflation; hawk; dove
13. unemployment; inflation
14. AD; unemployment; inflaiton
15. downward
16. unemployment; unemployment;
    unemployment; unemployment
17. inflation; unemployment
18. vertical; AD
19. true; labor

Important Concepts

1.

Event:	Change in money supply needed to stabilize real GDP	Change in money supply needed to stabilize the price level
The money demand curve shifts rightward	increase	increase
Investment decreases due to business pessimism	increase	increase
The government cuts taxes	decrease	decrease
World oil prices increase	increase	decrease

2. a. decrease
   b. increase
   c. no change
   d. decrease

3. a. shifts rightward
   b. shifts upward
   c. doesn't change
   d. increases
   e. doesn't change

4. An increase in inflationary expectations causes the actual inflation rate to be higher at any given rate of unemployment. This is illustrated by an *upward shift* in the Phillips curve.

5. A hawk policy tries to limit any rise in the inflation rate; a dove policy tries to limit any rise in the unemployment rate. Hawks and doves agree on what to do after a demand shock: neutralize the shock by shifting the AD curve back where it was. This will prevent any change in both unemployment or inflation. But hawks and doves do disagree about what to do after a supply shock, because any policy that limits the rise in inflation means higher unemployment, and any policy that limits the rise in unemployment means higher inflation.

6. a. unchanged target
   b. raise target

c. lower target (because consumption spending will decrease, which is a negative demand shock)

Skills and Tools

1. a. (See graph.); $500
   b. (See graph.)

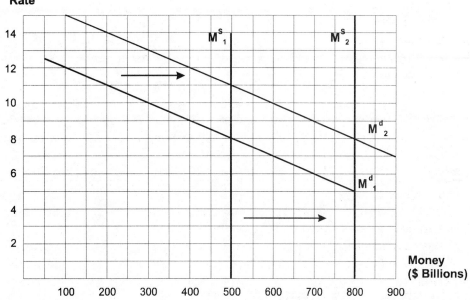

c. rise; decrease; shift leftward; fall; recession; increased; $800; (See graph.)
   d. Buy bonds! Buy bonds!; increase; increase; $300; buying; $120; increase; $800

2. a. $400; 7; right on target; $6; 100
   b. negative; leftward; fall; leftward
   c. (See graph.)

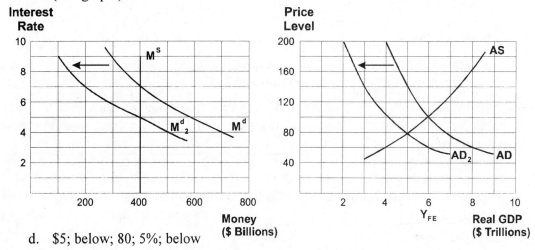

d. $5; below; 80; 5%; below
   e. new AD curve; fall further; 60; decrease; up; fall; leftward; *not* be the best policy

   f.   below; lower; increase; decrease; increase; return to full-employment GDP with a price
        level of 100
   g.   3

3. a.   3
   b.   demand; positive
   c.   rise; 22; upward; 5.5
   d.   down; rise; 7.5; 8; downward; lower; 5.5

15-Minute Practice Test

Multiple Choice

1. b	6. a
2. d	7. c
3. e	8. b
4. c	9. b
5. a	10. d

True/False

1. F	5. F
2. T	6. F
3. F	7. F
4. F	8. T

ANSWERS FOR CHAPTER 15

Speaking Economics

1. progressive tax
2. average tax rate
3. marginal tax rate
4. cyclical deficit
5. structural deficit
6. countercyclical fiscal policy

Chapter Highlights

1. nominal
2. income (or GDP); income (or GDP)
3. GDP
4. GDP; declined
5. military; military
6. Transfer payments
7. transfer; interest
8. fell; higher; decreases; decreases
9. upward
10. Deficits; Surpluses
11. transfer payments; tax revenue;
    transfer payments; tax revenue;
12. stabilizers; reduce; reduce
13. (nominal) GDP; (nominal) GDP
    (nominal) GDP
14. unified; social security;
    social security
15. potential (or full employment);
    potential (or full employment)
16. potential (or full employment);
    potential (or full employment)

Important Concepts

1. (any order): government purchases; transfer payments; interest on the national debt

2. Federal government purchases are spending on goods and services only; federal government spending includes *all* federal government outlays: purchases, transfer payments and interest on the national debt.

3. a. upward trend
   b. downward trend
   c. upward trend
   d. upward trend
   e. upward trend

4. (any order): timing problems; irreversibility; the Fed's reaction

Skills and Tools

1.

Year	GDP	Military Government Purchases	Non-military Government Purchases	Military Government Purchases as a Percentage of GDP	Non-military Government Purchases as a Percentage of GDP	Total Government Purchases as a Percentage of GDP
1982	$3,259.2	$228.3	$84.5	7.00	2.59	9.60
1983	$3,534.9	$252.5	$92.0	7.14	2.60	9.75
1984	$3,932.7	$283.5	$92.8	7.21	2.36	9.57
1985	$4,213.0	$312.4	$101.0	7.42	2.40	9.81
1986	$4,452.9	$332.2	$106.5	7.46	2.39	9.85
1987	$4,742.5	$351.2	$109.3	7.41	2.30	9.71
1988	$5,108.3	$355.9	$106.8	6.97	2.09	9.06
1989	$5,489.1	$363.2	$119.3	6.62	2.17	8.79
1990	$5,803.2	$374.9	$133.6	6.46	2.30	8.76
1991	$5,986.2	$384.5	$142.9	6.42	2.39	8.81
1992	$6,318.9	$378.5	$156.0	5.99	2.47	8.46
1993	$6,642.3	$364.9	$162.4	5.49	2.44	7.94
1994	$7,054.3	$355.1	$165.9	5.03	2.35	7.39
1995	$7,400.5	$350.6	$170.9	4.74	2.31	7.05
1996	$7,813.2	$357.0	$174.6	4.57	2.23	6.80
1997	$8,300.8	$352.5	$185.3	4.25	2.23	6.48
1998	$8,759.9	$348.6	$190.1	3.98	2.17	6.15
1999	$9,256.1	$364.5	$206.1	3.94	2.23	6.16

a. increased; more than doubled; No; the spending as a percentage of GDP
b. (See table and graph.)
c. are low and stable; decreased; 2.59; 2.23
d. 1986; 7.46; 1986; 3.94; 1999

e. increased; 9.60; 9.85; 9.85; 1986; decreased; 6.16

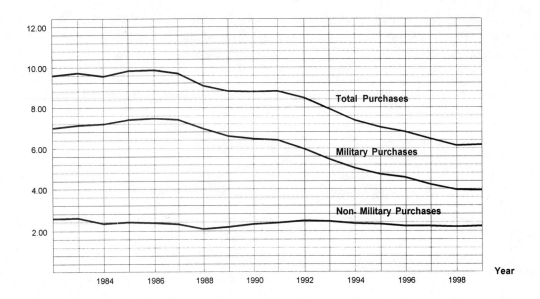

2.   a. (See graph)
        b. 4; 1.5
        c. demand for; rightward; exactly one trillion; a higher; 5.
        d. demand for; leftward; exactly one-half trilliona lower; 3.5

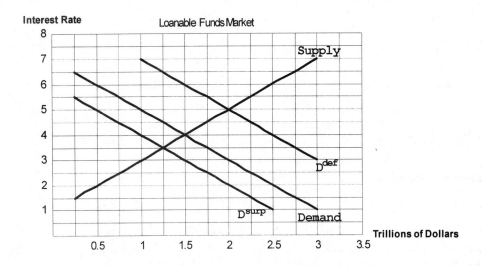

3.   a. investment spending; the stock of capital; shift up
        b. decreasing; demand for; down; a greater increase; upward; faster; more rapid.
        c. increasing; demand for; up; a smaller increase; upward; slower; less rapid.

4.   (See graph)
    a. higher; discourage; supply of; leftward; rise;
    b. lower; encourage; supply of; rightward; 9.

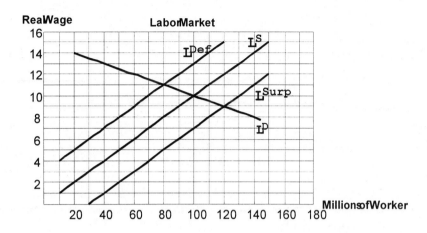

15-Minute Practice Test

Multiple Choice
1. c   6. b
2. c   7. d
3. d   8. e
4. d   9. d
5. d   10. b

True/False
1. F   5. F
2. T   6. T
3. T   7. T
4. F   8. F

ANSWERS FOR CHAPTER 16

Speaking Economics

1. foreign exchange market   11. triangular arbitrage
2. exchange rate   12. managed float
3. demand curve for foreign currency 13. fixed exchange rate
4. supply curve for foreign currency 14. devaluation
5. floating exchange rate   15. foreign currency crisis
6. appreciation   16. optimum currency area
7. depreciation   17. trade deficit
8. purchasing power parity (PPP) theory 18. trade surplus
9. arbitrage   19. net capital inflow
10. bilateral arbitrage

Chapter Highlights

1. exchange rate
2. buyers (or demanders)
3. sellers (or suppliers)
4. floats
5. appreciate; depreciate
6. short
7. short; depreciation; appreciation
8. parity; long
9. depreciate
10. bilateral

11. triangular
12. depreciation; appreciation
13. demand; sell; demand;
14. supply; buy; supply
15. above; increases; decreases
16. rise; positive; increases; fall; negative; decreases
17. stronger (or greater)
18. appreciation; decrease; more; increase; less
19. interest rates; higher

Important Concepts

1. (four of the following five, in any order): a decrease in U.S. GDP; a fall in the U.S. price level relative to the Mexican price level; a shift in U.S. tastes away from Mexican goods; a rise in the U.S. interest rate relative to the Mexican interest rate; and an expected depreciation of the peso relative to the dollar (or, equivalently, an expected appreciation of the dollar relative to the peso)

2. (four of the following five, in any order): a drop in Mexico's GDP; a rise in the U.S. price level relative to the Mexican price level; a shift in Mexican tastes away from U.S. goods; a drop in the U.S. interest rate relative to the Mexican interest rate; and an expected depreciation of the dollar relative to the peso (or, equivalently, an expected appreciation of the peso relative to the dollar)

3. a. dollar appreciates
   b. dollar appreciates
   c. dollar appreciates
   d. dollar depreciates
   e. dollar appreciates
   f. dollar appreciates

4. a. increase
   b. decrease
   c. increase (yen appreciates and dollar depreciates)
   d. increase

5. a. buy *more* of its own currency.
   b. buy *less* of its own currency.
   c. buy *less* of its own currency.
   d. buy *more* of its own currecy.

Skills and Tools

1. a. (See table.)

Currency	US $	Aust $	UK £	Can $	DMark	FFranc	¥en	SFranc
US $	1	0.5915	1.541	0.6674	0.4555	0.1358	0.009239	0.5753
Aust $	1.691	1	2.606	1.128	0.7701	0.2296	0.01562	0.9726
UK £	0.6488	0.3838	1	0.433	0.2955	0.0881	0.005994	0.3733
Can $	1.498	0.8863	2.309	1	0.6825	0.2035	0.01384	0.862
DMark	2.195	1.299	3.384	1.465	1	0.2981	0.02028	1.263
FFranc	7.364	4.356	11.35	4.915	3.354	1	0.06803	4.236
¥en	108.2	64.02	166.8	72.24	49.3	17.7	1	62.27
SFranc	1.783	1.028	2.679	1.16	0.7918	0.2361	0.01606	1

b. 40,700
c. 27,360
d. 108,200,000
e. 30,820
f. 14,905

2. a. (See graph.)

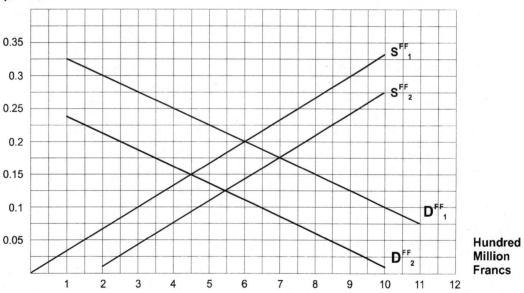

a. 4; 7.5; be exceeded by; depreciate; appreciate; $0.20
b. American demand for French francs; leftward; $0.15; (See graph.)
c. French supply of francs; rightward; $0.125; (See graph.)

3. a. $2.00; $0.5
b. francs; dollar-franc; 2,000,000; francs
c. pounds; franc-pound; 200,000; pounds

    d. dollars; dollar-pound; 400,000; dollars

    e. $300,000; rise; fall; fall

4. a. 0.175; (See graph.)

    b. decrease; increase; decrease; decrease; smaller; more

    c. rise; less; decrease; demand for; leftward; depreciate; appreciate; (See graph.)

    d. rises; more; increase; supply of; rightward; depreciate; appreciate; (See graph.)

    e. depreciate; appreciate; decreased; 0.175; 0.125

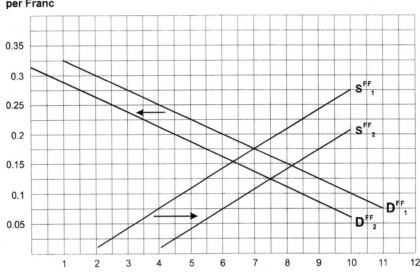

15-Minute Practice Test

Multiple Choice

1. e	6. b
2. d	7. b
3. c	8. e
4. d	9. c
5. e	10. d

True/False

1. F	5. T
2. T	6. T
3. F	7. T
4. T	8. T